PATH ILLOGICAL

A Memoir of
NYC and OCD

Nathan Kastle

S

Spective Press

The events and conversations in this book have been set down to the best of the author's ability. Some names and details have been changed to protect the privacy of individuals.

First paperback edition published
by Spective Press in September 2025

Cover Art by Ivan Cakić

ISBN 979-8-9994983-0-4 (paperback)
ISBN 979-8-9994983-1-1 (ebook)

www.nathankastle.com

In memory of Michael and Jeffrey, always.

Contents

PATH ILLOGICAL

1
Protecting Genius

The northbound express train barreled up the west side of Manhattan, carrying me along in its trembling hull to the Drama Book Shop near Times Square. The bookshop boasted the type of gentle, domestic lamplight that so rarely graced New York interiors. There, I got to be among fellow artists without being expected to interact with them and delve into plays without being required to finish them. I was traveling there from Bushwick to check off an assignment from my senior-year scene study professor, but I planned to get thoroughly distracted by whichever plays called to me once they were within arm's reach.

I watched as everyone aboard the train swayed and jerked in the same directions at the same time, as if we were a bucket of bait. I stole sacred glances at my fellow travelers. Two men in my train car descended into naps; one laced his hands over his gut and let his frown sink into his jowls like wet clay, trying to look threatening so no one messed with him while he was asleep. The other was younger and fought his sleepiness more acutely, as if telling me his stop was close without saying a thing. An attractive woman in her early thirties bookmarked the book in her hands, closed it, and straightened herself as she nudged her glasses up her nose. She seemed to be looking for something toward the top of the wall opposite her, but maybe she was just seeking to discourage the male gaze by feigning attention. I remembered women were not here to be understood by men; I moved on.

The ads above my head had been colonizing my peripheral vision the whole way, so I gave one of them a glance. The ad across from me read:

InsuranceGenius

Fuck, I thought. I looked away as quickly as I could, as if reading it was like catching an unpleasant eyeful of my grandmother in the nude. I looked straight down, and my bottom lip started trembling involuntarily as my heart inched up my throat. *Did that really just happen?* I thought. *I read the word* genius. *There's no way to unread it.*

The blood in my body gradually sank to the soles of my feet, and my eyes became distracted and jumpy. The train was no longer occupied by people of substantial interest; it was just filled with swaying, clothed bodies. I tried to stay still so as not to cause alarm, and I haphazardly assembled a strategy.

I turned my back on the ad so I wouldn't inadvertently read it more than once. *I need privacy*, I hissed to myself. My breath labored to enter my lungs like I was trying to stuff a scarf into a locked trunk. *Okay… I need to get off this train, like, now*, I decided. I needed solitude, yet I would settle for the Manhattan version.

I adored the concept of the word *genius* more than that of any other word. There was no limit to the power of anyone who fit the description of this word. But in the term's limitlessness, there was no easy path to defining it. Now, because I read it, every opportunity I would ever have to comprehend what genius could mean for me was being destroyed with every passing second.

I can't do it here. No way, I convinced myself. I knew what I had to do to solve my increasing dread. It just had to wait.

I tucked my chin, squeezed my eyelids shut, and griped, *What kind of insurance company has that word in its name? And how could I have possibly read it?*

I opened my eyes and lifted my head again. It was as though every person on this train now relied on the stillness of my facial muscles for a sense of general safety. Everyone would remain okay as long as I didn't reveal my inner panic or start my ritualistic response aboard the train. More rushing darkness crowded the car. I stared coolly through my agony, acting for the sake of my neighbors like I still had my wits.

The train's brakes engaged. The black shroud that had surrounded the train for a few miles was replaced, at last, with glossy, white-tiled walls. Then, the sight of people milling about in open space. This was the pat on the back I needed:

a station, any station. I waddled to the doors, lugging my numb feet with me. I widened my stance to stabilize myself as the train slowed. I faced the sealed door that would open any moment now. Any moment now. The train screeched to a stop, and I politely squeezed around the commuters and tourists as I broke through the open doorway.

The air shifted from the controlled climate of the train to the wild dampness of the metropolitan underground. With it, my mindset shifted to hare-brained urgency. I hunted for an area where I could stand apart and begin my rite. I found a section of the bumpy yellow strip at the platform's edge where I felt no prying eyes. I took a breath and let out a tiny, excited squeal that only I could hear because I had found a place to perform my inane observance without interference.

Before me was an expanse of black tunnel wall that would serve fine as the backdrop I needed for this process. Frantic laughs from a group down the platform sparked my instinct to look. Then, dutifully, I faced forward again. That was the last sound I would let breach my attention until I was done.

I felt similar to being on the pitcher's mound in Little League, getting ready to throw the ball. There was no external signal for when to throw it, only when it felt right. And I knew it had to come at some point. So I got my footing, reminded myself that I had to pose as though I was waiting for a train, and I began.

I conjured the image of four frames in the air in front of me—brown outlines hanging there in space. I focused on the first box. I bounced my line of sight within the box in the shape of a concave curve back and forth between the curve's endpoints four times. My neck took on the learned mastery of a conductor's wrist, and my head was the baton, precisely flicking through the air.

The first quarter of the ritual was nearly done. *This is to safeguard the meaning of* genius, I reminded myself. The word's ability to elude standard definition terrified me. Its significance to human welfare overpowered me. Now, any truthful meaning this word could have in my life would be lost to me if I didn't perform the rest of this procedure correctly and with appropriate vigor.

I usually performed this act in the comfort of my apartment. If I inadvertently encountered the word *genius* in writing or heard it said in a movie, I took the blow on the chin and resigned to sliding to the foot of my bed and drawing the shapes through the boxes against my closet door, uninterrupted. That was the usual way this procedure played out.

With breathless concentration and successfully resisting eyeing my neighbors to see if anyone had noticed me, I certified that I had completed the first box appropriately. Then, I brought my glance just below the lineup of frames and muttered what I always muttered at this moment in the performance, "Not *really*."

This phrase, the first time I ever engaged in this behavior, had felt like what I *chose* to say. Now, it was what I *had* to say.

Like a tightrope walker who couldn't afford to consider his ego or any other distraction, I brought my gaze to the second square frame. I began—

I felt someone's vision adhere to me from down the platform. I didn't even see them. I felt the sick trance they were in, staring at me. I darted my head straight to the person's legs with low, blue flames in my eyes and saw khaki pants. I wasn't willing to make eye contact with anybody just then, but I hoped my acknowledgment of the onlooker's lower body would discourage them from continuing to stare at me. I turned forward once again.

I beheld my dear canvas, but saw only a wall absent the four requisite frames. *Wait. Seriously?* I cried internally as I winced. *That person actually managed to break my concentration.*

This isn't right, I thought as I desperately pressed my tongue against my bottom teeth. I gave myself some moments of sweat-inducing repose. I had to wrap my head around how to restart the procedure, not appear insane to my neighboring travelers, execute it flawlessly, and maybe maintain some sanity. I tweaked my head to face a bit to my left and readied myself to pick the delicate baton up again. Then, I felt an unwelcome billow of air rush in from down the tunnel.

"Oh, fuck," I said under my breath. The train headed downtown—the one my body language was saying I was waiting for—was arriving. The black wall I needed was about to disappear. I hadn't considered that the train might veer into the station before I finished my duties. Turning away from the platform's edge, pacing around the benches in the middle of the platform, and all but twiddling my thumbs as I waited for the train to pass was a non-option. I pleaded with myself to remember the importance of what I was doing: *I'm responsible for preserving what* genius *means*, I reminded myself.

With the next exhale, I released all my pride. *Screw it*, I thought. I started swinging my head again like it was the lure at the end of a miniature fishing line as I faced the first box, copying the same lines I had drawn minutes earlier. The silver-bodied train squealed and hissed to a stop before me. *The walls of the train can be my new backdrop*, I thought. I didn't have that good fortune. The train doors opened right at my nose.

Torrential blue, red, and yellow flooded out of the train car. With some effort, I made the colors and motion my new muted backdrop. As frenetic conversation and laughter gusted through the doorway, I continued drawing my cardinal lines as subtly and accurately as possible.

The need to perform without error reached a crescendo as my shifting watercolor background did everything in its power to break my focus. I thought I saw a husky man with a large, blue IKEA tote bag slung over his shoulder. There seemed to be a panting dog lying down beside him. I made all signs of life an out-of-focus blur behind what mattered more: the four outlined boxes between my face and the train.

My hands started trembling. I made myself press them against my thighs. I made it to the second box for the second time. I slid my feet to my right to get out of people's way like a puppeteer was adjusting me. I completed the circuit through this box. I looked slightly below and muttered, "Not *really*," at a volume I believed no one could hear.

The recorded subway announcer stated that the train doors were closing. I spent a nanosecond appreciating that this was a good thing. The doors shut and locked. I swung my eyes slightly to the right to the third box. As if I were trudging through the thick mists of a nightmare, I made an upward-facing V, a downward-facing V, and placed two dots in the middle of each V with my gaze against the rushing train's body. I said under my breath once again, "Not *really*." The train rumbled away from sight, and my trusty black wall replaced it.

My face was a red-hot bed of embarrassment. I hadn't made eye contact with a single person aboard the train. I didn't even make the obligatory smile at the dog on the train floor, if that cluster of brown and white was even a dog. I didn't signal that I knew I was the same species as the others aboard the train. I just stood, offering no good reason for planting myself at the boarding area and not boarding the train.

I had come this far. It was time to finish.

My line of sight painted a large X in the final box, then placed two more dots in the upper and lower regions of the X. Then, as my calves quivered slightly, instead of mumbling any phrase, I raised my view to the upper right corner of my field of vision and let it hang there for a few seconds.

Then, I stepped off the mound. My puppet strings were snipped. I had finished.

I felt breath enter my lungs for the first time since reading the insurance company's promotion. The meaning of *genius*, though no more clearly understood, was safe for future use. I pivoted my body in a few different directions and located a sign with the station's name on it. I cautiously read it, convincing myself that it was highly unlikely to see the word *genius* on municipal signage, but one could never know. I finally identified where I was: Park Place. I was closer to the Book Shop than to my apartment, but I would have needed to board a train to get to either place. I was not ready for that.

I let out a deep sigh that I made silent by shaping my lips into a circle. My fingertips no longer vibrated from the threat of losing contact with my favorite term; they were numb as I slid them into my pockets. The ritual hadn't eradicated any of my anxiety. I knew this. It had condensed that billowing sheet of anxiety that had flapped in front of me all that time on the train into a dense, little ball that would pulsate at the bottom of my gut for a few more hours until mostly fizzling out.

I mounted the stairs back into the open air, where there were puddles on the concrete and glass installed in the sky. Maybe I ended up in a movie theater that night; maybe I crept through drugstore aisles looking for a chocolatey trail mix. Whatever I ended up doing, I spent hours mentally vacillating while trying to find my footing in reality. I was overcome with a sense that I had acted heroically by guarding such an important and esoteric idea, even though I didn't necessarily have to; simultaneously, I was mortified that I had spent so many minutes submerged in a behavior I knew was nonsense. As usual, the pride edged out shame to ultimately define my evening.

2
Treeless Apple

After I made it through security and into the terminal, I was greeted with grins as obvious as billboards by my neighbor, Christie, and my closest high school friend, Wyatt. It was a late night in mid-August 2014. We had separately traveled the forty-five minutes or so to the San Francisco International Airport from our hometown of San Jose, California. This was no seeing-Nathan-off ceremony. We all had boarding passes in hand. We had all accepted our offers of admission to the same school, New York University. Our parents, both thrill-ed and mourning our departures at once, came together for a tour-de-force ticket booking session that landed us all on the same flight.

"Think about it, bro," Wyatt waxed with big eyes on me once we got settled at the gate. He stretched his knees wide and leaned toward his fellow brand-new adults. "Nobody knows you in college. You can literally be whoever you want to show up as. It's wild, if you think about it. It's a completely fresh start." He was a six-foot-tall young man of Indian heritage with a highly Americanized style in all regards that I perceived: the way he spoke, how he spearheaded most conversations, even his name. He was serious about some traditional ceremonies and holidays he practiced with his family, but he hardly talked at all about them.

He scratched his neck for a while after he finished speaking. Wyatt had eczema, but since I didn't know anything about the skin disease, I always believed that his scratching was paired with moments when he was having an epiphany, as if the potency of his ideas came through his pores and made his skin itch. This was unlikely, but it always seemed to be so.

"Yeah, you're right," I replied, nodding with a quickly fading smile.

I saw myself posing as a haughty airhead who got everything he wanted, when I was rather a slim young white man with straight brown hair, deep pores, a large head, and a slight lisp. I tried to be aware of my privileges, but likely still abused them by taking many pregnant pauses I felt myself entitled to. (Which I now understand as luxuries because most minorities and/or poor people can't afford to spend time patiently thinking.)

I didn't make sounds of objection because Wyatt seemed to believe what he was saying, but I didn't buy into this "fresh start" thesis at all. No matter how much I would have liked to yank open the oven door and present a fully baked new persona, I could tell I would quickly become tired and return to what I was.

We lined up and funneled into the jetway. Christie lowered herself into her window seat, and my seat was right next to hers. Wyatt flashed his tongue and gave a hang loose sign with his hand as he waddled along in line and made his way to his seat somewhere deeper in the belly of the plane.

When we felt the aircraft's tires begin to roll underneath us, Christie and I turned to each other at the same time and made eye contact. Her excitement was so ravenous that her face looked like a happy balloon about to pop. Her eyes nearly closed as they curved into brimming upside-down crescent moons. She was restraining herself, but her joy was unmistakable. I smiled back, but my face felt like a purposeless piece of rubber that hadn't been manufactured into a product yet. All I was doing was what I felt expected to do: act excited.

I faced forward in my seat and stared at the hook holding back the gray tray table in front of me. The tabletop transformed into a ferocious lion wishing it could lurch out at me, but thanks to my hero, the two-inch plastic latch, it stayed in its place, growling, tamed. Then, I soberly reminded myself, *The latch is just there to control gravity and for safety... ugh. Boring.*

It felt like every being on this plane vibrated like generators, powering themselves and their families with raw alacrity; whether they were sure the flight would be pleasurable or that it meant mayhem, at least they were sure. I felt like a generator that was switched off. I gave the appearance that I was prepared, but I felt a lack of exactly what I was supposed to feel: radiating pride.

As the plane lifted off the tarmac, I closed my eyes and tried to conjure a beneficent vision of my young life, a synopsis of how I lived in the Bay Area. The first image that came to mind was the blue mountains. As a kid in Silicon Valley, I was surrounded by a horseshoe of blue mountains no matter where I stood. They beckoned like anchored clouds from a distant, serene wilderness. Before I understood anything about heavy smog and visual distortion, I just assumed my town was one of the few lucky ones that knew a horizon made of azure mountains as delicate as a vapor.

As hard as I wrung my mind to follow this vision with another relevant scene from my past, all I could see now was the pinprick of cabin light that permeated my sealed eyelids. I opened my eyes, disillusioned.

I shifted into the nook of the seat cushion. The small orange seatbelt icons overhead and little beads of blue light throughout the cabin against the dominating blackness created a constellation that allowed my mind to wander—my favorite state for my brain to be in. *I'm going to be a member of America's crown jewel city*, I thought, *a world-class place for artists to make it.* Wyatt was going to be a film major. Christie was going to do a pre-law course of study (which I understood nothing about). I let my head rest. There was no turning the plane around, no postponing the dates of orientation week as much as I itched for these scenarios to be plausible. I was going to be an acting student, continuing on my way to being what I wanted to be more than anything else: a respected actor working on reputable stages. I started imagining I would get some vaguely grand welcome once I saw New

York's dense glittering from the porthole window for the first time.

~~~~

After a forty-minute taxi ride through Queens during which I mostly noticed a few cemeteries and sparingly used basketball courts, we started crossing a bridge into the Big Apple. At the crest of the bridge, I could finally make out the first sights of Manhattan. They were brazen, vibrant street art pieces slathered over affordable housing projects stacked like boxes. As we reached the end of the bridge and entered the famed borough, my next impression was a discomforting one: *Man, there are no trees.*

The taxi came to a stop at a corner of Union Square Park. As we emerged from the cab, the contorted, eternal caw of the city breached my ears for the first time. The chugging of semitrucks at such proximity and sirens howling down the avenues made my chest reverberate. I heard squealing brakes, businesspeople on the phone, pods of girls chattering with each other. One sound stumbled into and amalgamated with another. Here I was, at the epicenter of the Coast I had never been to, and its soundscape was domineering and somehow symphonic. I thought of Rhode Islanders and Bostonians consciously choosing their towns over the heavyweight champ that was this place. It had to have lurked somewhere in the back of the minds of all East Coasters that they were either here or were not. And here I was.

I knew to expect the imperious buildings, but how they made me feel was surprising: both slight and slighted. It was not long before a slew of wailing ambulances came from around the corner that nobody in the city seemed to hear. Every ten minutes, another couple of ambulances or police cars came racing through the dense tangle—the prime example of New York emergencies not alarming a single soul.

Wyatt made himself heard over the din of the city. "This is so sick, man!" he said. "This is the place where almost every superhero movie ever filmed has been made. I can't believe this, bro." I looked over to the exuberant Wyatt. As he took in the metropolis, I saw the same sizzling wonder that was in his eyes when he spontaneously bounded over to me in the seventh grade and I had no idea who he was. He started giving me cinematic directions as an Australian filmmaker, beginning every directorial heart-to-heart with the phrase, "Now, here's your motivation, mate." I tried to join in the play as best as I could, but we were in the middle of class, and he just kept going. I thought he was off his rocker. This was how we became friends.

I looked back at the soaring walls of glass and the trails of harshly yellow minivans and hybrids that were like swift, beeping red blood cells that all but touched. I tried to relate to Wyatt's percolating thrill at being here. There was no easily identifiable hero rising above these millions of pedestrians to save the day. There was no equally identifiable villain thinking, from his twisted and power-hungry perspective, that *he* was saving the day. Whatever good and evil lived here was churning untraceably in the hordes of people.

I turned within to summon an image that could help me comprehend who I was at this moment, beyond a clueless young man meeting New York. The metropolis was raging with personality. *What is my personality?* I asked myself.

Well, I was the type of kid who, at the music store, filled my arms with fifteen rock CDs when I knew I had to pick just one to take home. I was that kid with my shins folded underneath me on the carpet, agonizing over the mosaic of albums that I created by spreading them out. Deep Purple, Stevie Ray Vaughn, Led Zeppelin, The Beatles, etc. If my mother had not compassionately asked which ones I could live without and thereby helped me ultimately pick out *Led Zeppelin IV* that day, I would have taken my hem-hawing to painful lengths and eventually been kicked out of the store by the shopkeeper. This memory arrived at a time when I was tasked with presenting myself as confident, yet all I could feel was reluctant acceptance and the slightest bit of charm that I was the kind of person who suffered over what mattered to me.

I was yanked out of my reminiscence by a puddle of urine splattered on the sidewalk we had to step carefully around. I fought to find some appeal in the persistent odors from stacks of trash bags piled like parapets on every block. I fought to see New York as the rest of the world saw it: the greatest city on earth.

We came upon a park. Seeing the sanctuary for rest and play was a familiar sensation from my childhood. But this park was distinct. There were bohemian twenty-somethings chatting, seated on blankets. There were people smoking, some openly, some discreetly, and a general maturity to the park. I let my ambulatory gaze settle on the forest-green iron fence surrounding the park. Without a strong reason to ask if we could stop and commune with the trees and feel the grass, I whipped my head away with forced disinterest. After I averted my eyes, I felt a stir of nostalgia. I gave the decades-weathered fencing a second look.

This time, I piped up, barely loud enough for my friends to hear. "This is where they filmed *Sesame Street*. Here in New York."

"Really?" Wyatt asked after a pause. He was quiet now and studied my face, likely seeing a contained glee in me. "That's what you see, bro? Huh!" His "huh" expressed the passion he felt whenever trying to traverse the gap between his perspective and mine. He never shrugged me off. The ideas of those he considered his brothers, like me, always merited his most sincere interest. But perhaps my comment made him think about his earliest memories at a time when he was just starting to sculpt his new identity. We spoke no more about *Sesame Street*.

Nevertheless, the dignified fencing around the park aroused dormant memories of some of my favorite segments of the show. *Sesame Street* ferried me from many crusty-eyed early mornings into a more knowledgeable and resplendent state. In the segments filmed at parks like this one, Grover, the furry blue puppet, stood in for an adult and guided kids through interviews or let them lead the conversation. And now, we were passing this space. I was bitter that the whole city wasn't a park, or maybe I felt shortchanged that the dignity of the play space was so dwarfed by the fact that it was behind us so quickly. I straightened my back and braced myself. Time again for steel structures owned by corporations and concrete filthy beyond measure.

I watched Wyatt and Christie soak in our new home. They looked at it like it was an ornate hotel lobby that just kept welcoming us and impressing them. But to me, New York was soaking *us* in. It was licking me up and down like a bear cleaning its paw. We had selected a school whose campus was not a campus. Our learning environment was this: the stern grid of effervescent avenues and lanes. New York was nudging me and hinting that I was an adult now. I tried to learn the lesson the way it was coming, but the tone in which it was delivered was grating.

Christie, Wyatt, and I formed a small triangle on a corner that was quieter than some others when it was time to part ways and move into our three separate dorms. Our pod of mutual understanding that was delicately intact during our flight and taxi ride was already well into decay. We all readied ourselves to carve our disparate paths that would lead us through college and adult life.

Although I would have loved to continue beholding the spectacle of my friends' faces eating up our new pinball game of a city, I had to walk my path. I aimed in the direction of my dormitory building and hurled myself through the nettle. The path took me past halal food carts with steaming flattop grills in tiny stationary trailers, African soap peddlers with desperate eyes and uninterested in giving any spiels, unhoused pregnant women in tears, volatile drunks, and several commercial professionals with places to be and wins to make. I finally reached Palladium, the former concert hall converted into my new residence, and stepped into its revolving door.

The sky I had known all my life was vast. The best quality of the suburbs had nothing to do with its many KFCs and nail salons, but that it was under a magnificent, pure sky—the same sky that was over other, more wonderful places. It was a sky so powerful I had to squint just to look at its open blueness whenever lying on my back in a field.

Here, my eyelids did not have to strain. The tops of the mammoth structures sliced the sky into jagged shapes less luminous than any sky I'd ever known.

I heard a middle-aged man in passing say to his friend, "Only tourists look up in New York City." I forced my chin down after catching that. I detached my awe from the metropolitan feats of architecture and invested it instead in the bobbing heads in front of me and at the sidewalk under my feet.

I was inside now, for the first time since JFK airport. The Palladium lobby was bedecked with glossy chrome surfaces under a lofty ceiling. The security guard even wore a black tie on a white button-down. I got into one of the four elevators and got off at the eighth floor. When I entered the room I was assigned, I saw a six-foot-three, mixed-ethnicity young man who looked like a personal trainer with a slender waist and strong deltoids putting his clothing away in a dresser on the half of the room he claimed before I got there.

He took a good look at me, then gave a broad, goofy grin and reached his hand out.

"Hey, man, I'm Hudson!" he said loudly. As I leaned in and shook his hand, I saw in his eyes that he, like me, had very little street smarts about our new environment. But that is where the commonalities withered. The consequential difference between him and me was that he excelled at pushing charisma and confidence through every pore on his body. His feet met the floor more nimbly than mine, because he was always bobbing like he was a butterfly getting ready to sting.

Our hands parted. A nuanced but unmistakable display danced across his face: slight movement in his brow, a widening of his eyes, followed by a twitch of his lower eyelids. This all communicated to me that Hudson intended to assert himself as alpha. I had never considered snatching up a status of superiority in a relationship with another guy. I never had to. Then again, maybe neither had he.

From the eighth floor, it felt like someone left one of the tall windows open and swirling clouds came in, obscuring my vision. They obfuscated what was valuable and what was unimportant; what was real and what was artificial. Deciding these foundational aspects of my collegiate life felt like decisions that were meant to be made by someone else; how could I find the power and courage to decide my own path forward? There was no way to do that without stepping on some toes or stepping into what I saw as unacceptable stereotypes: the white guy with privileged bravado; the smug, funny know-it-all. Nuance was the dream, but it felt just out of reach. And I didn't know why.

There was a mandatory floor meeting that evening organized by the two RAs on our floor. I remembered Wyatt's remark about the opportunity for rebirth as a college student as I took my seat in the enormous circle. After thirty or so people spoke, it was my turn to introduce myself. I told everyone where I was from, what I was studying, and my fun fact was an anecdote from my college essay, the odd fact that I once offered a dozen donuts to a Buddhist nun and she declined. I found it not only taxing to present myself as someone new, but I had to exert myself to present who I thought I already was. My fun fact landed limply compared to the riotous ones that came before mine. I took more time to think about my answers to the rest of the getting-to-know-you questions during my turn to speak than others had.

All my floormates were bursting at the seams with personality, their self-confidence as robust and healthy as Michelangelo's *David* is beautiful. If they were nervous, they manipulated their nerves to come across as cute or charming. I was realizing I relied on a stoic disposition to communicate my seriousness as a first-year acting student. When I had to improvise answers to silly questions in front of a group of students from around the world, I turned inward. I felt this was the smartest move until I feared it was communicating exactly what I was trying to hide: my anxiousness.

I strode out of the meeting room and back into the network of hallways on the eighth floor that awaited me. I had heard the stray phrase "New York can chew you up and spit you out" in the elevator just before the meeting. Would this formidable town pick me out of its teeth like an older man at a diner? As I walked down the hall to my room, I concluded that I was to rise to the occasion of succeeding in the underbrush of this jungle. I was to join the ranks of the giants who made this city and this university as legendary as they both were: Martin Scorsese, Robert De Niro, Billy Crystal, Donald Glover, Anne Hathaway, etc. I stepped into my unadorned, safe bedroom and wondered, *What if I fit into the gears of this city like oil and turn out better than how I arrived?* I determined I was going to be a success story. I had to be.

I saw my nighttime view from my window for the first time: Third Avenue and a staggered row of apartment buildings. I saw a hundred little windows illuminated, behind all of which were people telling themselves, *I'm going to be a success in this town. I have to be.*

3
Sibling

When my mother was in her early forties and coming out of thirty years of education to be a psychologist, she was called out by a coach of hers for "observing her own life" rather than living it. She took the criticism to heart and felt deeply called to become a mother before she lost her chance. So, she pleaded with her partner at the time, a man named Karl who worked for the newspaper of my hometown, the San Jose Mercury News, for a baby with a small nose and a big vocabulary like his. Soon after, he presented her with a paper coupon for one baby, on which he wrote "irrevocable, non-transferable."

With a mother who was deeply invested in my existence and a father who recognized her desperate yearning when he saw it, I was conceived. The expectations around their dynamic, as in, if it was a relationship at all or simply a child-creating agreement, became hopelessly muddled after I was born. My mother wanted the family. My father wanted to present his coupon and enjoy watching my mother redeem it, and didn't want much more beyond this. My mother and father split within a year of my birth.

I saw my dad one day a week on Sundays. The two women in my household, my mother, Rhona, and sister, Libby, felt that I was already a good little man in my early years. They admired my natural sensitivity and saw my gentle nature as a great asset.

A female village raised me. These were my mother's friends and all their daughters, more than 10 women. I learned more about feminine power than anything about myself from the time I was born until I was four. Though the support was as sweet as pie, neither my family nor my village could embody an exemplary masculine persona for me to work toward.

I needed an example from a man. I went into Sundays with Dad having the unspoken preconception that providing an example was what all fathers were for.

As soon as I turned six, I understood that spending time with Dad was a voluntary activity. So I examined the phrases he chose to say, and adjusted to the laidback frequency in which he lived. I got used to his focus on keeping me entertained. What I was scouring for were tidbits of value from him.

When he picked me up in the early afternoon and leaned in for a hug, he was solid and toned under his old, heather gray athletic shirt. His torso smelled like brewing coffee and stale Marlboros. He walked me across the street to his 2010 blue Jeep Liberty.

Once I was around nine years old, he started forming the fabric of our relationship on a Sunday afternoon by unspooling the question, "So what's new with you?" I quaked in my seat. I had an excruciating time answering this inquiry. *What's new?* As I know now, *everything* is new to a child. His conversation starter was likely just that—a starting point. The question was never intended to make me suffer, but I suffered over it. He made several shots at the breeze. It was as if he didn't understand that to me, he was the breeze.

Almost every Sunday, he and I ended up in a movie theater. As the trailers played, I wished I could be facing my father instead of the screen. I had reveries of his lifestyle as a graphics editor at the San Jose Mercury News and mused about how he spent his weeks. I had no method for asking him about himself because he rarely asked about me in the language I understood.

I wished to have nuanced, emotionally vulnerable exchanges with my father every now and then. Say… as we played chess or snacked on nuts in front of the TV? I yearned to have those profound whispers between two men that no one else in the world needed to hear. A talk about what we each valued? About how to set goals? How to start a conversation with a girl? Perhaps generational differences clouded the line of communication; both of my parents sought not to inflict the direct damage, both emotional and physical, that their parents inflicted on them.

When he wrote on his chunky laptop, which was often, he never talked about what he was writing with me. Was it a secret? Was he just not aware that what mattered to him mattered to me?

At my fourth birthday party at a waterpark, I was surprised with a foster sibling against the splattering of fountains against pavement. While my dad unboxed a bike he gave me and wrestled it to the ground to assemble it, a little girl younger than me with a round face and long, unkempt blonde hair was seemingly conjured as if my mother had cosmic powers. My mother whispered something to her, probably along the lines of "Say 'hi' to your new brother!"

I was perplexed why she remained standing there, staring at me. She was two years old. She looked at me like she wanted to hug me, but held herself back while she looked down. *Who is she?* I thought.

When my mother met Libby and heard her story—the abusive foster mothers, the neglect of Libby's basic rights to joy and freedom—it was as if my mother had to adopt Libby, as if she was profoundly compelled. My mother saw no other appropriate response than to include her in the family. I would applaud her heroism if it were not for the fact that *I* was Libby's sibling and she was mine. Becoming a sibling with a girl who did not share my blood was an experience I was never prepared for.

My mother eased herself into the presumption that I was a lonely child, like it was a sofa, and seemingly never got up from that mindset once she was comfortable. My mother never asked me how I felt about becoming a big brother. I had never known any feeling like loneliness in my first four years. I felt vitalized from my own curiosity, thrilled at my freedom to play and learn, and able to amuse myself with my propensity for thinking ravenously.

It was a wonderful experiment playing with Libby at first. I noticed key behavior traits about her, like her clumsiness and her brash and fiery attitude. I knew these were not my own qualities because they were so innately inverse from how I felt, but I was constantly on the verge of forgetting she wasn't me. I soaked in her distinctions gratefully and embraced knowing nothing of myself at the same time. Together, we made a game of scouring department store floors for knick-knacks and scraps. But I felt a tension, perhaps spiritual exhaustion, from playing with someone who made me feel that there was no choice but to love her. I fell in love with observing her more than loving who she was.

After months of her shaking up the home, I finally asked my mother what was with her extended stay. "Mommy, I said, "when is she going home?"

My mother smiled at me, softly sighed as she looked up at her eye level, then told me as she looked down, "Sweetheart, this is her home now."

Dong. Dong. An ominous knell pealed throughout our townhome.

She's staying here forever? I thought.

I knew then, at five years old, that this relationship was going to demand a lot of observation and egregious patience.

The differences unsettled me further, if not deconstructed me. Libby's front teeth were larger than mine. She lied to Mom often about sneaking candy or money. She was exemplary in love and wrathful in war. She was born with an impudent transparency that neither my mom nor I had. I became hopelessly entangled in the question of *how* she could be related to me and what being a brother meant.

I needed to be the best brother I could if I had to be her brother; that much was obvious to me then. When I was old enough to realize that there were thousands of other kids out there and Libby was the one my mother chose, a thought entered intrusively: *Would this happen with another kid? Will someone else also stay for the rest of my life?*

Some days, I didn't want to be her brother. I couldn't accept that there was room to grow into myself alongside her. Because she was close, she demanded my attention. She didn't watch as closely as I did, so if I relaxed into the unknowns of my journey and thought about myself instead of the one that I could always see with my eyes, would that hurt her? Wouldn't that be a pointless endeavor, to pursue happiness instead of service? I was confused, but I was sure of myself.

Dong. Dong.

I remember the aesthetics of my own thoughts from this era more than I remember the design of the wallpaper in our bathroom or the shape of our kitchen chairs. My cerebral landscape usually felt like a New Mexico vista of shallow hills rolling in authoritative silence. Or, it was obfuscated with shadows like a boneyard, with the occasional granite monolith that burst from the foundation and towered above the rest of the thoughts: *why is she my sister?*

Nothing mattered more than figuring her out, including learning how to love her in a healthy way. I insisted that if I just found a great reason as to why a girl who did not share my blood was my family member, then maybe I could try becoming my own person, apart from her. But in my crazed search, I lost track of where she ended and I began. My natural propensity for compassion overpowered my capacity for self-regard.

When I was about seven years old, Libby and I were going to bed for the night. She had the larger room even though I was older. She scooted into her room, cooing, "I love you, Nate-Nate!" I hooked a left into my bedroom. From my chambers, I could only muster the day's final, honest word. "Thanks."

Sometimes, timing can get muddled with intentions, and impact can misfire when one is suffocating at one's own hands.

As a youngster, I saw that teachers were our guides, the ones who deservedly did most of the talking and harbored wisdom that they worked on releasing to us every day. Yes, there were a bunch of little kids in my first-grade class, but they didn't yield much wisdom. They may have brought some fun, but the teachers were the endlessly generous souls.

I enjoyed making paper airplanes with other kids and throwing them into trees that grew great, brown pods. I also liked inventing games in the school's field with others. I competitively read a book about dragons with one of my pals. But these kids… they kept. Coming. Back.

Because they were near, my emotional habits and muscle memory kicked in. Because they were near, this meant I had to love them. My peers were fixtures that mimicked Libby's constancy. The similarities were haunting. If I weren't careful, my buddy Jimmy would be the next little kid to take away all my life force; If I spent too much time with him, I would end up funneling all my care into his soul like oil into a bottle, with nothing left for myself. I considered the consequences of intimacy to be obvious. Somehow, most people powered through. But socializing was a commodification of myself. Eye contact—that obligatory gaze into those expanding, shrinking, and assessing organs—meant digging into my pockets to find personality coins. Once I spoke my mind, it meant handing out those coins. I knew how coins spread far and wide; I felt I would never see those parts of me again. I had no term for *intimacy* as a youngster, but I was no stranger to being terrified of that facet of my life. I loved people. But my love was as distant as it was searing.

During a lunch break while I was sitting at a table by myself, my mom (who was volunteering for the school that day) asked me why I wasn't playing with the other kids in my grade. I replied, "I enjoy my own company, Mom!" And I meant it. I was nowhere near an outcast; I was well-liked. However, I derived more enjoyment from thinking about other people than I did from partaking in the risky trading of parts of myself that was inherent to interacting with other kids.

I sauntered through the sprawling field of my elementary school, imagining that several floating, voyeur cameras were pointed at me as I walked. Each camera captured a different angle of the same one-man reality show, the premise of which was me walking and thinking. These floating recording devices were live-broadcasting my behavior to an audience of one: my crush at the time, a red-headed girl in my class whom I considered an angel. As the cameras observed me, my awareness of my thoughts and my movement made them feel more precious. I took on greater care just from knowing I was being watched. Having an audience brought more tension, but I simply felt more life coursing through my veins from it as well. It was a completely self-originated belief and a strong one: I could endure any hardship as long as someone or an audience of more someones were there to watch me live through it. Viewership was next to salvation.

4
Performative Tendencies

I unknotted my tie and started to rub makeup remover into my face after the weekend's final performance of *Twelve Angry Jurors* (a stage adaptation of the film *Twelve Angry Men*) in my senior year. I played Juror Eight, the role Henry Fonda had in the film. In the dressing room, I hooted and twittered about the show with my friends, including Wyatt, who was a crew member on the production. As we celebrated a job well done, I glanced at my phone for the fourth time since stepping off stage.

I had already been rejected by most of the schools I applied to, though I had gotten into Chapman University in Southern California and my so-called safety schools, a state college in Southern California, and a small university in Long Island.

I clicked the button to open my phone's screen, and I saw the notification for an unread email. The subject line read, "Your NYU admissions decision." I felt my chest go vacuous like I had no heart, and then my torso was beaten from the inside like the skin of a drum. I opened the email. I skimmed through the message white-faced and slack-jawed, and then I found it: the word "Congratulations." I darted my eyes through the body of the email, rereading my name—just to be sure—and read the beginning of each paragraph: "Please know that you were considered for any and all programs… as with all of our admissions offers, your admission is entirely contingent on the successful comple-tion… Nathan, you have every right to be proud…."

"I got into NYU!" I screamed to my friends, breaking into paroxysms of relief.

Wyatt joined in the frenzy. We both started jumping, then haphazardly embraced and beat each other's backs. Wyatt had gotten into NYU's film school weeks earlier because he had applied Early Decision. He submitted a short film that he and I created. I was elated and incredulous that our brotherhood would continue for four more years into college.

I muttered, "excuse me" to no one in particular, then bellowed and sprinted into the courtyard right behind the back door to the theater. I lay flat on my back on the blacktop, alone, still in a full suit. I stared into a blank night sky as I caught my breath. The sky mostly had a brownish hue from the light pollution of my town, but a couple of stars shone through. As I ran my fingers over the loose pebbles on the ground, I said four words to the stars: "I'm going to NYU."

My high school put on the play *Deathtrap* by Ira Levin in the first semester of my sophomore year. It's an intimate thriller, with five cast members and most of the stage time shared between my character, an up-and-coming playwright named Clifford Anderson, and the playwright he idolizes and whose home he is invited to, Sidney Bruhl.

The effulgent lights made my every thought and expression transparent and conveniently shrouded the audience in a radiant fog as well. I stepped on stage. I loved that there was no room in the psyche or on the stage to hold back and play small. It never occurred to me that this was a way to express myself. It was an act of service, of inhabiting another person and representing them with truthful life.

I gaped at props from Sidney Bruhl's plays once I was invited into his home, but as the actor, I was staring at the red boxing gloves of Jake LaMotta from Raging Bull. That was how I was able to nearly faint from the thrill of holding the flails and axes from Sidney's plays as Clifford.

Nearly every night we performed, crew members and fellow actors told me right before I stepped on stage, "Remember to have fun!" I internally rolled my eyes. The encouragement to enjoy myself was well-intended; I understood this. But this was my chosen lifestyle. I spent hours studying the script for *Deathtrap*, chipping away at understanding and then embodying what my character was *doing*, given only what he was *saying*. During my free time backstage, I pantomimed pushing a grocery store cart and putting boxes and bags into it, so I could step on stage having just come out of doing something, rather than initiating behavior out of nowhere.

Acting was a submersion into an alternate life—a fresh beginning for me, yet a dunking into someone very much so in the *middle* of living their life. I was thoroughly aware that I had the power and responsibility to represent this other person with vigor. Acting was always about more than having fun. When I stepped onstage, I bloomed into a fuller being.

At my NYU audition, which took place in a hotel in Los Angeles, my monologue deliveries were nerve-ridden and felt forced. It was my interview with the admissions officer after my monologues that I felt sealed my acceptance into the university. The gentleman behind the table asked great questions. I detailed what theater meant to me—the immediacy of the exchange between performer and audience, for one—and what I thought theater could become in the future.

I spoke about something I didn't even know existed—site-specific theater. I detailed visions of theater breaching into public life, creating performances in the middle of public spaces, and hooking the busy executive on his way across the plaza by simply creating art and existing at the same time. I articulated what I saw as the power of young people to shape this unbounded art form and the power of the art to deliver its young people to a more disciplined way of life. While my heart was skipping beats left and right and my mind was a rapid cyclone of desire and self-doubt, I dropped the pretense and sturdily stood in the eye of the storm. I let the unadulterated passion I had for acting flow through me as authentically as I could.

When I left the room, surprisingly, my heart rate went back to resting—this was the feeling of having represented myself as well as I could and leaving nothing unsaid.

My mother advocated for me to go to the acting school of a decent university in Southern California, which I was accepted into as well. I told her that that route felt like "chasing my mediocre dreams." I paid little mind to the immense tuition bill I would rack up at $35,000 a semester for the eight semesters I planned to be a student there. When it was decision-making time, she told me she could handle it. She gave me a big hug and giggled as she told me to follow my big-time dreams.

My placement in one of the ten studios that make up NYU's drama department was a consequential decision that was out of my hands. The first two years in NYU's drama department were called "primary training." Students studied at one studio for two years, having all their bad performance habits from high school and unhelpful artistic ideas demolished with a caring touch. After year two, students then had the choice to remain at their original studio for "advanced training" or to move to a new studio that taught a dramatically different philosophy of the craft.

I got the email a few months after my acceptance into NYU: I was placed in the Experimental Theatre Wing, or ETW. I immediately took myself to the NYU website, my anchor that clarified the university's goals for me and what I could expect from being a student there. The description was minimal and what was to be expected: sentences about open-mindedness and trusting the student to decide their path through the program. I then went to the Tisch School of the Arts Class of 2018 Facebook group. There was a joke circulating there that sought to describe every studio to a tee. The premise asked, "How many ETW students does it take to screw in a lightbulb?" The answer? "Purple."

The time came to begin my work at the most mysterious studio at NYU. It was time to smear purple paint onto my cheeks and wear tattered garbs or whatever they did there, and begin with no clue what I was in for.

5
Experiment

We were all shepherded by a few professors into a circle so massive that our backs touched the cracking teal paint on the walls. We sat on the hardwood floor in a circle vibrating with gregarious energy. I was mystified by how voraciously people were talking, purging their own stories and gorging on others' before the assembly had even started.

"Hey," a biracial Latina to my left said gently to me. "What's up? I'm Moriah. What's your name?"

I was startled.

"Oh, hi." I smiled at her. I failed to remember what she said; I was so harpooned that she said anything. "Sorry, what's your name?"

"It's Moriah."

I gave her my name. I kept my smile floating on top of my apprehension like an apple bobbing in water.

It hadn't even occurred to me to introduce myself to the people whose knees I almost touched with mine. I couldn't believe these students were comfortable being seen as people who didn't have anything figured out. I heard them joke about just that while I hid that I shared this with them. I was awaiting what I had waited for all summer in California: I wanted the professors to do the talking. I wanted the mystical heritage I was sensing in the worn and welcoming space to be put into words by those who had been here for years already.

The studio's director stepped into the clearing inside the wide circle. She leaned forward when she spoke, as if needing to get a message across a long table. She was so titillated and honored to be speaking to us, her eyes were opalescent golf balls. She wore a polychromatic shawl that looked like a find from a market stand in Thailand.

She spoke of getting out of this program what we put into it. She spoke of finding groundedness, a oneness with our bodies. She told us this was a safe space where we would find other folks exploring the marvelous unknowns that were within us and discoverable through collaboration. We were encouraged to open our hearts to their fullest extent, after which point the faculty would guide us on how to stretch them further open. The director ended with, "We do not teach experimental theater. The curricula themselves are an experiment."

Woo-hoo, I thought sarcastically. This introduction to the work was sounding hellacious right away to my intellect. Whatever cerebral tendencies I had, they were going to be challenged here. But this was the new home of my ambition; here on the smooth hardwood floor, a floor imbued with decades of passionate pounding from honorable past dancers and actors, I rested my heart. This was a new artistic home pitted against my natural tendencies to want peace, simplicity, and safety. Not a chance of any of the above here.

We had a Linklater technique voice class that lasted eight months. In three of those months, we focused exclusively on how to breathe into different parts of our bodies. We learned from the get-go that ETW placed little worth in an "I" that we conceptualized outside of the body. All that we were, all that we were going to become, was housed in this body. Even still, we also learned this body was not our only body.

We were taught by the genius Lisa Sokolov in her Embodying Voice class that we have physical bodies, emotional bodies, energetic bodies, and timeless/knowing bodies. We were taught that we had the rare power to *know* that we had rare powers.

In the Linklater class, we began with four months of the devotional study of our breath as it showed up in our bodies. It was a voice class halfway into which we had not yet used our voices. That was how they wanted to build us: to give us a strong foundation of breath in our bodies. We breathed from one spinal vertebra at a time throughout dozens of hours in the studio. Every single hour of this class's actual content was spent with our backs or stomachs on the floor. The floor wasn't just smooth from being danced on for a certain amount of time. It was imbued with palpable energy entrusted to it by fleets of budding artists. I was grounded. I was present.

As I lay on my back, feeling myself breathe from my pelvic floor rather than my lungs on this particular day, I formed the unignorable image of a shared consciousness with my fellow students, which looked like an energetic umbrella hovering over us as we breathed.

Having empathy for others doing their self-focused work felt like a contagious bug I had caught. I couldn't help wondering what it was like for person X and Y to roll their bottom spinal vertebrae against the floor as they breathed slowly and deeply, while I did just that with my body.

I wanted to be great. My search for greatness was less a desire and more a piece of my self-image. My trajectory toward mastery of myself was of the utmost importance.

I felt betrayed by the classmates around me because they were doing exactly what I was doing. How could I be great, how could I stand out, if all our bodies basically functioned the same way? How could I reasonably believe that the way I breathed made me stand apart and hint at future success? I couldn't.

I felt threatened by this umbrella of collective consciousness that bound us. I didn't credit myself with creating this idea; I felt it was entirely imposed upon me. So, as I tried to apply merit to the sensations of my organism, the body that was my livelihood as an artist, I was resentful that I wasn't in a private lesson. My potential was being robbed from me because my peers proved my breath was nothing special.

We only studied in the studio three days a week. We plunged into the black depths of our deepest hopes and spiritual mysteries in our studio. We elicited truthful responses from our scene partners, we had unexpected outbursts, and cathartic crying fits. We experienced artistic progress that was beyond what I thought possible.

Then, on Tuesdays and Thursdays, we had to pack up our bags with textbooks and commute on foot to various NYU buildings around Washington Square Park. I felt like the undead, tucking away the achievements of the heart I had discovered in studio and listening to a bland academic teach comparative literature or introduction to physics. This body that was cracked open like a golden egg at ETW had to stuff itself into a folding lecture hall seat all day, for two days of the week. I felt the need to feign some naïveté that there wasn't creative magic inside me, so I could focus on taking notes in my academic classes. Living a double academic life as an experimental artist and a test-taker was confusing. My academic requirements were not why I came to New York, obviously.

Our contact improvisation class in ETW began with the foundations of the practice: we all warmed up our bodies in our own ways for twenty minutes, then we sat in an enormous circle. One person entered the space. They didn't walk, they experimented with their physicality and different body parts, often staying close to the floor like a freewheeling amoeba. Then another rolled or oozed or inched into the space to join the first experimenting body. The practice is centered on the minuscule and rich moments of the two bodies (then five or six later in the work) coming into contact with each other. To me, it was the art of honoring touch.

Then, in one class in week three, we were asked to leave the building. We were invited to disperse independently and explore the neighborhoods surrounding the Tisch building: the East Village, SoHo, and Greenwich. The instructor asked us to take this excursion (which lasted until the ninety-minute class was over) in complete wordlessness. Silence. We were encouraged to listen to every sound we could hear—both the dominant and the more nuanced ones. I walked toward SoHo. I heard the clanging of an American flag's pulley against its pole, a shopkeeper sweeping water from the front of his shop, passing phone calls coming into and leaving earshot, vehicle tires rolling against the pavement. I ran into the one and only F. Murray Abraham. I just looked at him as he was talking to a friend outside of a business plaza, and then I kept walking because there was nothing I was meant to say.

This exercise made me feel the sun's rays more articulated on my skin. I roamed a city that was as unknowable as it was beloved by most of its inhabitants. Surrendering myself to silence was not completely foreign to me. Something about being encouraged to do it felt like a win, a charitable contribution from the professor to my power as an artist.

In every ETW class at some point, we students sat barefoot on the floor in a circle. Being barefoot in the circle wasn't required, but there was an unspoken understanding, at least to my mind, that those who kept their socks on were holding something back, not embracing the emotional nudity that was required to benefit from the lessons here more fully.

That was not about to be me.

I went to the ledge where we placed our belongings, like water bottles, backpacks, and coffee cups. I was a slender, gentle young man who nervously anticipated what it would feel like to release myself from the shackles of undefined experience and put words to the process here. This was an opportunity that mattered to me. On cue, my nervousness was rattling viscerally within me.

The instant I decided speaking in this circle was an immense opportunity, I involuntarily looked for ways to guarantee the impending joys or surprises I wanted to find in the circle.

Somehow, I needed to certify that the delicate event of having an explorative discussion would go as well as I hoped it would.

I dropped my socks onto the little ledge, which was essentially the interior sill of the wall of windows. *Oh, shit,* I heard myself think. I dropped my socks in the exact incorrect spot. Where the socks were placed did not matter—I knew it then and I know it now—but because the reality had become that *this* was the spot where my socks landed, the site became nightmarishly inappropriate.

The place they landed was going to guarantee the opposite of what I wanted: now, I would flounder in the circle or not say anything at all. Fearing this drove me to do what I did next: a kind of act that I thought would revive the scenario in which I would be articulate in the circle. Still, I was unsure about what to do.

What are you doing? the thought came in. *Adjusting your socks is not optional; it's critical so that you can be ready for whatever shape this talk will take. Don't be a fool. Move. The. Socks.* Before I did, I legitimized my nonsensical movement by rifling through my backpack for nothing at all with one hand. With the other hand, I used my finger's knuckles to slightly nudge my socks to a new position a couple of inches away from the horrible spot. I raised my body, and the apartment buildings across the street that were visible through the glass suddenly were surreal. They looked like they were vacant or merely an object of my imagination.

I knew now that there was no point in having moved the socks. This made me panic. Why did I do something completely illogical that served no purpose? Then, I picked up the socks and placed them in a third place and promptly trotted over to the circle.

I sat down.

Shit, I thought. Now I suddenly needed to ration my eye contact with my peers because I needed to grab hold of something real, but couldn't stare. Then I realized that depending on watching their eyes as a reference point for reality was not slowing my inflating worry. I returned to my body for answers, thinking I was following the wish of every faculty member here. *This must be what it feels like to be an individual*, I thought, disappointed that only at the height of my panic following an inane protective behavior did I get the wake-up call that I was alone.

My sock-adjusting behavior was an act I couldn't imagine anyone else caring about. So, if it was all mine, the optimist in me reasoned, it had to serve as a clue that I could achieve the greatness I craved all alone. If I not only survived this illogical behavior but was the only person in the room concerned about it, this really was the body that would carry me to my creative success. It was tangled logic, but I was encouraged by it nonetheless.

I ended up internally mulling over the tension between the bizarre and redemptive qualities of the sock-adjusting, instead of freely ideating and sharing like I hoped I would. A technique I thought would help me be more courageous sapped all my courage instead. There was an impenetrable wall between my open mind and the open talk. Maybe people were waiting for the guy with slightly anxious energy and a lot happening on his face—me—to say something. No one knew I had crushed any likelihood of ideating freely by engaging in two consecutive panicked and illogical behaviors.

I owed it to myself to speak from my heart and express how deeply my love for this art spread, and I owed it to them to communicate how lucid my respect for these peers of mine was, and how strongly I believed in the nascent creative paths they were forging. What they got was someone who suffered over how he moved his socks. They got the version of me who internally twisted my predicament so that I found pride in my pain.

I shaped my eighteen-year-old identity not so much by testing and tweaking socially, but more by radically exploring my kinesthetic sense of self. I became known in ETW for my passion and prowess for movement.

In movement classes, we were just as frequently invited to improvise material in front of the class as we were to share choreographed dances. I ate up both opportunities like I could subsist on the craft of movement.

I only sporadically let my breath come out of me to verbalize ideas; I more often felt it vacate my body in a huff as I dipped my hip down with a foot reaching in the opposite direction. My breath was sucked back into me as I stretched my fingers and kept my eyes on them. Then I looked away, waved my arm like an octopus's tentacle, then looked back. I shot myself into the air. I articulated my wrists and fingers at an angle away from my face, physically making a calculation of the air around me.

I was heavily influenced by Buster Keaton, the silent comic who was, in my opinion, wrongly less famous than Charlie Chaplin. He told epic, unforgettable stories with an unwitting, stoic face as his body performed feats of unprecedented scale.

My other great influence was my idea of how villagers in Mesopotamia, the world's first civilization, would have moved. I used the body as a tool to communicate, in geometric shapes and languid, soft expressions alike, as if I were moving before words were here. I moved as if I were an inventor before any other inventor.

Dance was not just a niche I felt comfortable in; it was a calling I acted upon. To say my strained relationship with my peers informed how I moved would be an understatement. When I performed in movement classes, the flow was for them. I, a pitcher, poured myself into the twenty-five glasses that were my attentive classmates.

Not everything I wanted to say was communicated through dance, but I felt no need to say anything else after I danced.

6
Explanation

I left the Tisch building for the day. I walked through the city back to my dorm in the bronze, late-afternoon light. I had no choice but to trust New York City to hold me as I stumbled into it in spiritual fatigue. I was tender as I braced against scammers pushing blank CDs onto unsuspecting passersby. The setting sun was only visible as I crossed any given street—a pretty inopportune time to appreciate a sunset. The way the sunset was always obstructed by a block's buildings or flanked by miles of shimmering windows made me feel that the sun belonged to New York City, as if it had a patent pending on the celestial body.

I was halfway to my dorm (and, in fact, near a city park that may have gotten my wheels turning) when I realized I had a yearning to do something very specific. This urge felt like a controlled flame that was present throughout the day at ETW. Now, in my privacy, it raged into a bonfire.

I wanted to explain myself.

I was learning that acting could be defined as the art of behaving truthfully under imaginary circumstances. Furthermore, I was learning that it was difficult for any actor to learn the craft by approaching how to "behave," so for our intents and purposes as students, the definition of acting breaks down to *doing* truthfully under imaginary circumstances.

For someone dedicating my life to the art of doing, I knew that what I wanted to be doing in my personal life was strange. But I couldn't help it; the warmth from the fire was too overwhelming. I wanted to *explain* more than anything.

Why hadn't any of these peers of mine asked me, "So, Nathan, what's going on up there in that noggin, bro?" I was ready with an answer: "Well my sister is really on my mind a lot, because I never had a say in becoming a brother, and I feel a lot of parallels between being forced to love someone because they are near me and the qualities of the social dynamic here at ETW." I was locked, stocked, and loaded, ready to introduce myself in a way I saw fit.

But no one ever asked me to explain myself.

Of course they didn't. I reluctantly understood: everyone was themselves. They had plenty else to focus on.

On my walks back to my dorm in the plum-colored dusk light, I started pondering the etymology of the word *explain,* without pulling out my phone to supplement with any research. I toyed with the word in my mind as the sun settled under the horizon: *ex-plain*. I chewed on it. *Hm. Like, ex-plane. So, that's like removal from a plane,* I deduced. *Explaining is removing oneself from the plane of existence. So,* I continued, *if explaining is an action made only in a detached space where people remove themselves from the field of reality to come up with good explanations, my desire to explain myself is totally misguided.*

First, I was excited to have put my finger on the action I most wanted to take. Then I picked at what mattered to me and stripped it of all validity through further thinking. I was confused, but at least I was sure of myself. Explaining was not the way after all.

The first step of socializing always appeared to be barbarically claiming a seat at the table by barking something unimportant just to participate and get one's foot in the door. I shuddered at the prospect of talking over someone else just to let people know I did have a pulse and wanted to get to know them. I could sense when I had the chance to participate and concur, "Maple donuts are the best!" I let myself have the thought of what to say, and I kept the thought bound within. Without knowing it, I was hoarding social output because I reasoned that college was for learning and the post-graduate world was for investing actual energy.

I starved myself by how strictly I limited my understanding of what *learning* meant. Learning was done at the behest of a professor. Period.

NYU's website didn't promote making friends in college, and the university website was how NYU wanted to be comprehended. *So, there's no way that outside of Hollywood, there's any real value in making friends in college. Aha.* Another conclusion reached sans external input.

In California, I formed a perfect image of vague, solemn acting students milling through the halls at ETW, always rehearsing lines so they could be ready to step on stage at any moment. Despite my wishes for my concept of these faceless students to somehow materialize here at NYU, I was instead presented with a messy, diverse, fascinating array of who was actually there. I mistook the lush bouquet of souls who attended NYU with me as the perfect curse. It was Libby all over again. Because they were near me, I had to love them. That was the only kind of love I had ever known since Libby was adopted: love required due to proximity. Here, it was the inverse. Proximity was chosen because of love.

I couldn't understand the camaraderie here. I listened so carefully to others' lunchtime conversations in the lobby that I could have been physically leaning in for all I know, not saying a word, so enraptured by the most basic exchanges. The more I listened, the more I heard vapid topics being brought up. Over burritos and salads, one girl mentioned *iCarly*, and a second girl grew excited because she loved that show six years ago. Then both of them noticeably put a cork in their excitement because they knew there were other works of art more worthy of their worship. The third person in the group piped up and said, "Have you guys seen the 2004 film adaptation of *Phantom of the Opera*, though?" Then the three of them fawned and laid their arms on each other in celebration of a film they all loved so much it hurt.

I wanted no part in it. I rationalized that the conditions to make friends at NYU were too imperfect for me to bother. I figured I was only here for four years, so I would just make friends after college, where it wasn't so conflicting with the fragile trajectory toward success that I was responsible for maintaining and which I kept close to my chest. I saw what my peers were creating as a turbulent and fickle lifestyle. It seemed like a life of ogling over the scripts of *Hamlet* and *Rent* and talking about the work casually, rather than performing it or preparing to perform. This constant chit-chat about childhood summer camps and artistic giants in the same sentences... this couldn't be how they prepared to perform, could it?

I couldn't see myself embracing my mortal cluelessness as expressly and expressively as they did. How could they stomach baring truths to one another after only having met six months ago?

I further ruminated that if I were on the road in a van and stayed at a commune in Vermont for a few nights, then I might find my people. If I released into social vulnerability while officially affiliated with New York University, a nightmarish image barraged me: I feared the NYU emblem (a violet torch in a violet rectangle) would be branded somehow beyond my skin and muscles and straight onto my forearm bone. Logically, I knew this wouldn't happen, but the fear of having an osteal mark from NYU was severe. If I made love in this private university's buildings, if I had the best times of my life as a registered student, I would spend the rest of my life owing a privately owned institution credit for my best years. The school would continue to torment me for years after I graduated by rendering me the only one who knew I carried the silly but permanent brand.

I'd never had such an irrational fear be so dissuasive to me. Other fears had dampened my courage before, but never the image of a white-hot brand stamping my bones. My technique for avoiding this was to rely on myself rather than the resources provided by the university as much as possible.

Social circles collected and flowered in the ETW lobby before classes, between classes, and after classes without fail. On the off chance that I did initiate a conversation with a peer, it was rare that it didn't include or begin with a genuine compliment. I revered these artists and was terrified of their might all at once.

I felt that socializing with other ETW students off-script was to hand them pieces of myself, like playing cards, that they couldn't be trusted to return. I feared the likely danger that everyone was handing their cards to me, too, in the swift and steady exchange of love that happened in the studio's halls. A successful future was in my hands, and socializing reminded me that my fingers weren't webbed. So I guarded my hope for my future that much more strictly.

After we bared the unrefined corners of our souls for everyone to see in class, and as the social circles clustered in an uninhibited snap, I looked for a way out.

I smiled warmly at whoever lifted their head to look at me as I headed toward the stairwell out of the wing. My smile was a guise. It was an adamant goodbye masked as a delighted hello. Community was a terror, a body collective with the kind of gravitational pull that would have me dropping my playing cards and losing touch with who I was.

These thought tendencies were tightly wound around my spine since I was a boy, like warm copper wire. I never questioned my perspective that interaction that wasn't guided or structured was a threat to my personality. That was just how the world was.

7
The Sight of the World Behind Me

I stepped out of the shower in the morning as the spitting image of exactly what I thought my peers wanted from me: to be a delicate and dedicated supporter, giving them space… but perspicacious.

Presto. I was ready to be at the studio, the environment where the opportunity to become friends with my peers lived. If only I could teleport my body in this blissful state directly to the Tisch building. But there lived a city that had not known a tranquil moment of quiet for centuries. My path took me from the Union Square neighborhood, south on Broadway, and had me arriving at the Tisch building, which had ETW on its second floor.

I entered the thrashing river of Broadway. Filthy concrete was underfoot, and a horde of people behind me and in front of me thrust me forward, while a parallel horde moving in the opposite direction passed me by.

No lanes existed.

Vigilance was required.

I did my best not to step on a slower walker's heels; I also sought to avoid walking face-first into someone and doing the inadvertent tango from left to right until we finally got around each other.

Coming across another face was a momentous occasion. It always had been and felt like it always would be. I couldn't understand how so many millions of living souls in such proximity to each other could commit to essentially ignoring one another and the fact that, together, whether they knew it or not, they were shaping culture and exemplifying astounding diversity.

Everyone who wasn't sobbing, coughing, yawning, or laughing with a phone stuck to their face just appeared so ambivalent. Couldn't this clean-shaven man in the forest-green sweater vest and vintage dress shoes see that he was rubbing elbows with dozens of potential mentors, investors, even spouses... and that he could be a vital role model himself? Couldn't I say the same for myself, in my blue tie-dye T-shirt with a psychedelic guitar graphic screened onto it that I liked because it expressed my inner flamboyancy when my quiet usually led the way, wearing my five-inch-inseam, black cotton shorts that were favorable to wear in the studio?

I remember walking down the street grinning. I remember people looking at me. I often nodded to them or kept looking forward, making my grin a spectacle that was complimentary and easy for me. Then I couldn't keep it up, the grin.

So, I made a show of holding my smile back. I hoped what I was doing was unmistakable. With my cheek and lip muscles trying to invert my smile, I hoped to communicate that I felt forced to act ambivalently toward everyone, while inside I was calmly glowing.

I couldn't fight the knowledge that these people were sublime potential friends. I fell in love with potent passersby.

I passed what I categorized as "fixtures": things like subway station entrances or a storefront's sign. I thought of these fixtures as proof that there was a real universe beyond the mind. These were physical solid accumulations of molecules that almost every human could point to and agree were there. In my reasoning, this gave all the more merit to the minds of all these people. If we could all agree that a Capital One bank was at the corner of Fourteenth and Broadway, then what other magnificent, more abstract ideas could we also agree on?

I wanted to burst out at someone who caught my eye and stop them: "Hey! Yes, you! What's on your mind? Pardon me, let me back up, what's your name? What are your dreams? How close are you to them? How much do you suffer? Do you have the kind of dreams you feel the need to write down in the middle of the night? What was something funny your kid said this morning over his eggs? Let me reiterate, how much do you suffer? How happy are you?"

A Latino contractor, wearing all-white overalls with brown paint splattered on his clothes, lumbered up to me. I noticed he had deep folds around his eyes, *either from squinting at the sun or laughing,* I thought. Then, he vanished into the chasm behind me that felt like a boneyard of every person who became an instant muse.

Five or six people after the painter was a young, sullen guy in wide-legged corduroy pants and a loose-fitting tee. He raised the volume on his wired earbuds with one hand. I looked into his eyes while he looked straight on. He raised his hand to the hair that fell into his eyes, then he was gone into the abyss.

Why not just turn my head around to check in on those I'll never see again, those I'm losing the chance to know with every moment?

I turned my head over my left shoulder, still walking.

I saw everything as if looking into a refrigerator after a long time, where everything was orderly and just as I had left it. I saw the humongous marquee above the movie theater, the sales racks outside of the famous bookstore, and the vague, haunting power of the backs of all those heads. I turned my head back around because I had to see where I was going.

Seeing the world behind me was like approaching a masterful painting. The longer I stayed with it, the more subtle memories it stirred in me, and it made me feel aches and pleasures I was not feeling before I laid my eyes on it. The obvious question arose for me: Why did I bother looking behind me when my head naturally faces forward? Because the world behind me was unprovoking, serenely familiar, and had a million little parts and people that I knew I missed the first time approaching it.

I let out an absent-minded chuckle. Turning around on Broadway imbued me with the settled confidence of a kingpin. The present moment was spastic and volatile: it kept birthing new city blocks every few seconds and choking me with a thick, white vapor of a million unknowns. *Why don't more people look behind themselves while they're walking?* I wondered.

I knew nearly every great mind touted the present moment as being the residence of all living beings, and therefore crucial for us distractible humans to be aware of. The way I saw it, I had no choice but to live in the present moment. So, I could spend some of my time turning my head over my shoulder to see the past while the present cocooned me.

The human stimuli were endless. A commercial executive clacked her designer heels against the pavement; a modestly dressed man with a puffy face who seemed like a good guy came out of a coffee shop and hurriedly stuffed his wallet back into his pocket as he reentered the stream; a stout mom of two held her children's hands as they stumbled along in tow.

It was time to play my trump card. I intentionally stepped down with my right foot so I could rotate my head around as far as possible.

I looked. There it was. And there they were.

But I felt differently this time. Everything was still there, but it didn't present like a museum exhibit. It just felt staler.

I received confused eye contact from the man walking directly behind me in the same direction as I. I turned forward again to ensure I didn't walk into a sign.

Still, a stark relief rippled through me.

I turned my head around at least another five times before the half-mile walk was over.

I laid my hands on the staff-like iron door handle to Tisch, and that's when I knew. I was here.

Everything I had done to feel better about being in class, namely turning around while walking forward, would now prove its efficacy.

Weeks later, the head-turning became just like the banks and stop signs that I cherished for their obviousness: the behavior was a fixture.

I no longer looked behind me to follow up on friends who left as quickly as they came. Whenever I envisioned myself in class that was about to start in fifteen minutes and felt anxious, I stepped down on my right foot and... did it. I was promised security by this behavior, and it delivered spurts of confidence. It gave me a sense of immunity to surprise. Then that feeling faded, so I had to bet on turning around again.

I never forgot the disapproving eye contact I had shared with the man walking behind me in my direction. He looked at me like I was defecating in front of a police car. Whenever I looked behind myself in the weeks that followed the first instance of my head-turning, I upgraded my game. I committed to the guise that I was looking for someone I was supposed to meet, whom I had reason to believe was behind me. That was the performance.

Not only did this diminish some of the confusion in the man's face, but it also allowed me to scan the city behind me for longer. I had to make it to class, and perhaps more importantly, I had to be ready. Maybe even numb to surprise if I could help it.

And apparently, I could. This was my version of doing my best.

Months into performing this behavior between Union Square and Washington Square, the head-turning brought spikes of satisfaction that were sharper and shorter-lived. Immediately upon twisting to face forward again, I felt horribly hollow, like a vacant cathedral with no one to appreciate its ancient beauty. I was resorting to this technique so often that it had to have a purpose... *Right?* I asked myself.

When I finally asked myself if my habit was helping or hindering my ability to succeed creatively and socially, I didn't know how to answer. I had no idea.

The anomaly of this habit was unsettling me.

As I was one prone to constantly calculating my potential and measuring my distance from meeting it, I refused to ignore this conspicuous sign of disturbance. I was lucky to detect that this was not a joy, nor even an act of will. It was an interference of some kind.

No one else was making me do this, and I didn't necessarily want to keep doing it. But I couldn't quite stop.

I had a hunch about where to begin to look for answers. I wasn't playing around when it came to figuring this out. I decided to look into any possibilities that occurred to me once I returned to my dorm one evening in November.

At the top of my mind was OCD—obsessive-compulsive disorder. I had only the most basic common knowledge of this disorder, but one of its qualities stood out to me as being possibly linked to my experiences: the repetitiveness.

The repetitiveness.

There were other clues that something was awry with my lifelong ability to "be good" and "be chill" (these were the hallmarks of wellness, according to the colloquial terminology of Bay Area high schoolers. "You good, bro?" was the essential way to check in with a friend. "Chillin'" was the standard response). I was losing touch with these faculties fast. One of these other hints arrived as I fell asleep.

When I was ready to call it a night, my phone was usually the last thing to leave my hands. I placed the phone on my desk. I got into my bed. Then, as I tried to fall asleep and enjoy being unconscious in slumber, I was prodded by the sense that I had placed the phone incorrectly on the desk. I opened my eyes, and while still lying in bed, I picked it up and put it in a different spot on the desk. I tried again to fall asleep. Anxiety gurgled in me like boiling milk: I hadn't found the perfect location for the phone on my desk. I repositioned it several times, an unwanted nighttime practice that soothed me not. I continued this pattern until exhaustion overpowered my need for perfection, and I was able to doze off.

8
Common Knowledge

My father and I stopped at the home of a friend of his from decades ago when my dad and I were in Phoenix, Arizona, during a road trip through the American Southwest. What the two of them had in common was years spent in a Christian cult, his experiences with which my dad wrote about in a memoir. His story was one of years as a missionary under a deranged and dangerous leader.

My father must not have had much of an impression of how this woman, the friend he had a trauma bond with, conducted her private life. She opened the door, and we gingerly entered an excessively cluttered home. Her living space was lined with stacks of boxes that reached the ceiling. We had to walk the paths she had carved to clear space for the uncommon visitor. She went to fetch us drinks and apologized with a ducked head as she scuttled around. I noticed that an apology about her space wasn't really what she was expressing. She was mortified, yes, but without plans to change her ways anytime soon.

She had to touch the light switch panel three times before turning on or off the light. When I made eye contact with my father, it was usually at the side of his eye as he was thrown into the outfield by what confronted him here. My father and she found a place to sit around the detritus to reminisce about the good days they shared.

My father pulled me aside as night fell and whispered that he didn't want to stay the night here, even though those were our plans. He realized we would only embarrass her if we ducked out of our commitment with no good reason, except that we felt secondhand discomfort from her lifestyle.

Sleeping under her roof was a vaguely oppressive experience. I lay in bed, fearing that she might scold me if she saw me turn on a light switch without doing it her way. She was forthright when she told us herself that she lived with OCD. She talked about it openly and with that ducked head again, like her condition was just like any other trait a person might have, i.e., charming, shy, nervous, obsessive-compulsive.

I gathered only the bare minimum of common knowledge about obsessive-compulsive disorder as a kid—for instance, it could manifest as repetitive handwashing that felt necessary to people who had this disorder. The television series *Monk*, starring Tony Shalhoub, who plays a detective with obsessive-compulsive disorder, also introduced me to scraps of understanding about OCD. These were ten-second snippets before I changed the channel to find more pleasurable entertainment. Tony Shalhoub's body language reminded me of that of a rodent squirreling away food for the winter. Except his tension wasn't momentary, he was in a visceral self-protective and anxiety-avoidant mode at all times. I switched the channel before thirty seconds lapsed every time I came across this show on television.

I didn't know anxiety was involved in the picture with OCD at all, much less that it was one of the driving forces behind the urge to complete a compulsive ritual in the first place. I had no idea OCD was considered an anxiety disorder at the time (in 2013, the American Psychiatric Association reclassified OCD into its own category, Obsessive-Compulsive and Related Disorders, in the DSM-5).

This was not a disorder less understood than others because it had a minuscule impact. It was a disorder that was concealed masterfully by its sufferers and misunderstood by most, except their therapists. Shalhoub wasn't squirreling away any food; he was combing through consecutive and unending obsessive thoughts.

On the day in November when I finally questioned the reasoning behind my head-rotating, I actively responded that evening. I wasn't good at asking for help, but I also was not one to ignore a potentially substantial obstacle in my path. So, I improvised baby steps. I capitalized on some privacy I had while my roommate was out, sat at my desk, and opened my laptop. I typed in the search bar *symptoms of OCD*.

I clicked on the first result, which took me to the website of the International OCD Foundation. I skeptically wondered what they hoped to communicate with their elegant and modern pale blue logo of the letter "O" with the letters "C" and "D" inside it. If there was an entire foundation dedicated to spreading awareness of and promoting the treatment of this disorder, what was I about to walk into?

The page for the International OCD Foundation began with the header "What is OCD?" I read what was below: "Obsessions are unwanted, intrusive thoughts, images, or urges that trigger intensely distressing feelings. Compulsions are behaviors an individual engages in to attempt to get rid of the obsessions and/or decrease distress." My eyes opened wide. I summoned to mind everything I had been doing and avoiding, which led me to this online search in the first place. "Holy shit," I said to myself softly. *Maybe there's something here*, I thought.

Further down the page was another statement about obsessions that stood out: "Individuals with OCD do not want to have these thoughts and find them disturbing. In most cases, people with OCD realize that these thoughts are illogical." *People with OCD realize their thoughts are illogical? And they do the compulsions anyway?* My arm hair raised. *Is that anything like me?* I genuinely wondered.

I rose from the chair. I paced to the window overlooking the twilight city below. But the view was not demanding my attention at this moment. I paced back to my laptop and put my cheeks in my hands as I closed my eyes tightly.

I thought of my mom. If she were here, she would have softly instructed me to seek help. She is a psychotherapist, primarily for addicts and trauma survivors. I was often frustrated that she consistently advised me to seek help from someone else, rather than encouraging me to find what I sought first in myself.

Had mine been a milder case, I probably would have done nothing about my habits. But my place in the city was starting to feel like a severe mismatch. Massive, tangled ropes with giant knots in them matted the ground and forced me to tiptoe and crawl prostrate through them to make my way.

I opened a new tab. My online journey now took me to a registry of therapists who specialized in OCD. I picked out three and called the first.

"Hi, Dr. Layton," I began, stepping in a slow circle around my room. "My name is Nathan Kastle, and I saw your profile online, and it says you accept NYU insurance. Well, I'm an NYU student, and um," I stopped my pacing and looked up. Just a white ceiling. I squared up with the concept I knew I had to put into words: "I've just been noticing, um, some kind of strange behaviors I've been doing, and I guess I'm just calling to find out if I may have OCD." My face became flushed as I put the words "I" and "OCD" in the same sentence for the first time in my life. I gave her my name and phone number again and ended the call.

9
Not Your Average Bear

The office was the width and length of a matchbox. I felt no claustrophobia in Dr. Layton's office, though—the slim window brought in more light than seemed possible. Plenty of light always put me at ease. Considering the circumstances, I was only partially relaxed.

"So, what brings you here today?" the therapist asked me with utter openness as she sat down.

"Oh, uh…" I pressed my lips together as I thought. I immediately felt a pressure to perform, the same feeling I had on stage, but less exciting. I'm not sure why. Maybe it was because her gaze was so genuine. I sat in her large blue armchair with my hands pinned under my thighs. As I began to craft, or rather, piecemeal an answer to her question, my eyes were drawn to the abstract art on the walls—broad, light gray brushstrokes crossing over narrower dark gray brushstrokes. On the opposite wall was a framed quote that said, "You don't have to believe your thoughts just because you think them."

"Yeah, so, basically, I've just been noticing that when I walk to class, I've just been starting... this habit of mine where I'll... look behind myself as I'm walking, for whatever reason, and it's just getting kind of annoying." I coughed it up like a hairball. I detested being so unsure whether I was just a random guy off the street who had no reason to be there (and was wasting both of our time) or if the opposite was true.

"Right," she said, welcoming me to elaborate. I did not. "Okay." Her eyes were keen and small, almond-shaped as if whittled by years of closely studying her subjects. She had pretty, shoulder-length, wavy red hair.

She had a slight New York accent; her voice wasn't necessarily soothing like the voice of my mother (the therapist I had known for the longest time), but it was strong. However, the tone with which she spoke demonstrated great care. She crossed one leg over the other and leaned forward as she carried on the conversation. "You mentioned over the phone that you study at NYU, right?" she asked.

I nodded proudly and meekly all at once.

"It's a great school," she said, eyes directly on me.

"Yeah. Thanks." I smiled.

I was craving the carrot dangling on a string in front of me throughout the session. I had no way of knowing if my prize was to be found at the end of Dr. Layton's legal pad or in another doctor's office. The carrot was the answer to my question: did I or did I not have OCD? Was I wasting my time, or was my self-perception about to change?

"So I'd like for you to have a sense of the kind of people I work with," she said as she opened her palms and then rested them on her lap.

Though we were both there to work on me, I nevertheless waded through a marsh of presumptions of what I imagined was going on in *her* head. Whether it was because I was fascinated to be in the company of a New York professional who wasn't directly linked to NYU, or I was compensating for my discomfort, or both, I couldn't help but reflect, *How challenging it must be for any therapist to have a first session with a patient.* I scrutinized the little expressions on her face as she studied me. I thought, *She has to prove she has control over the interaction and has expertise, express a genuine interest in my case, and introduce me to the ins and outs of this disorder, all while listening closely to what I have to bring into the room.*

"I work with all kinds of people," she continued, "from all walks of life. I've worked with individuals with OCD for about twenty years. Several people that you would never suspect live with this disorder. Celebrities, teachers, parents. My patients have repetitive, unwanted thoughts that they do not want to have." She was teaching me gently and genuinely. "OCD is a cruel disorder, it really is, and people don't understand that. It will make you create habitual responses to these thoughts that people like my patients get stuck in. These are behaviors that OCD makes up in order to get rid of the anxiety or distress from this unwanted thought. Someone with OCD will end up repeating and repeating these behaviors, called compulsions, not because they want to, but because OCD clouds their judgment to assess what is safe and what is unsafe. They will perform a compulsion to be absolutely certain. And it's impossible to be absolutely certain of anything."

I let out a chuckle. I thought Dr. Layton was joking about being unable to be certain about *anything*. She kept a straight face and observed my chortle. Maybe my laugh wasn't a great sign. Maybe it was a good sign. *Whatever, keep listening,* I told myself. I tried to funnel my scattered attention back on her.

"*Did I turn the stove off?* Plenty of people have this thought, but they can let it pass. Someone with OCD will check, then check again, because the disorder prevents them from being okay with being unsure. It also has the power to… if a patient stares at the switched-off stove's dial for five minutes, they will walk away and still think it's on. OCD creates tremendous doubt.

"Most of my patients come to see me because they need help to stop doing these behaviors—these compulsions—that have taken so much from their lifestyle. They want their lives back. And our work gets them back to living. Is all this making some sense so far?"

"Yes."

"Great. So that's where our work comes in. I work in a type of therapy that's different from traditional talk therapy, okay? That's not what we'll do here, or psychoanalysis. That has been proven to be ineffective in treating OCD, which many clinicians don't know, but that's another story. It's sad, but—anyway.

"I work with a therapeutic style called cognitive behavioral therapy. This form of therapy offers some perspective on the distressing thoughts someone with OCD has by intervening at the behavioral level. So, with CBT, cognitive behavioral therapy, it's a model of what we experience in our minds that we can work on: thinking, feeling, and behavior. Our work is like a sub-section of CBT: a technique that seeks to prevent the compulsive habits by exposing you to your anxiety and getting you to a place where you're okay experiencing anxiety before you can push it away and engage in the compulsion."

I watched her, shy and fascinated. She was studious of me from the moment I walked in and didn't let up with her razor-sharp observational skills. I felt she was intent on fostering a zero-judgment zone where I could feel as free as possible to share my experiences with her. Not only did I see it in her eyes, but I also felt her lack of judgment. I felt the cushion of the armchair under my bottom, my feet on the floor, and it no longer felt like the seat I was invited to sit in ten minutes ago was going to swallow me whole. I removed my hands from under my thighs and placed them in my lap.

Despite feeling gradually increasing comfort, I felt from the moment I opened my mouth in her office that I was quite rotten at conveying my symptoms or even identifying what they were. This was going to present an issue if I didn't get better at it.

"Together, we begin to confront someone's fears. We approach them head-on and work with techniques to start living with the anxiety that these intrusive thoughts bring— just living with the anxiety."

She was a graceful speaker. She seemed to have found her life's purpose in helping people somehow apply courage to an illogical and frightening disorder. Her clientele sounded somewhat like me: people who often doubted their own knowledge, thoughts, and behaviors. Her efforts to make me feel completely comfortable in her office were equivalent to her pushing a boulder uphill. But I noticed it was her goal, and I appreciated that.

I was relieved she was nothing like the last therapist I saw when I was fifteen. My previous therapist often finished a cigarette at the last minute before our weekly sessions began. When I came to him, citing an inexplicable fear that felt parasitic and present in many areas of my life, he explained that we are programmed with fear so that we run away from the venomous snake that's about to bite us. He didn't get the hint that my fear was more excessive than the instinctive mechanism.

"So it sounds like you are experiencing some repetitive behaviors, and these are behaviors you don't enjoy doing?"

"Yeah, pretty much." My eyes switched between looking at her and her shag rug as I described something I hadn't described to anyone else at this point. "And, like, for example, if I make eye contact with someone as I'm looking behind me, they might look at me like I'm doing something totally crazy, and I really don't... enjoy that."

"Are these new patterns of behavior or something you've experienced for a while now?"

"More new."

"More new." She echoed and made a note on her pad.

Dr. Layton wasn't just planning on sending me home with a poem recommendation to finalize the treatment, which is what my prior therapist did. She was interested in getting to know me. This meant a great deal to me. I also loved that she didn't appear to be the least bit self-indulgent. *Maybe I picked a good therapist*, I thought, and I felt a bead of light spark in my chest.

"I've always felt like there's one right way to do something. And my mom thinks that's pretty peculiar... but I don't, like, have problems with washing my hands too much." I thought I was speaking her language by bringing up handwashing, and she would signify recognition. She did not.

She studied me over her rimless glasses as I spoke. My energy was fraying, and my inner organs were doing a hectic hora. I was almost entirely concentrated on how I might be negatively affecting her. I willfully focused on vacuuming my emanating aura from the air to feel secure and small.

I looked at the clock. We were about halfway through the fifty-minute session already. I had learned a good deal, but frustratingly, I still had no idea if it was relevant to me.

She opened a manila folder on her desk, pulled a stapled packet from it, and handed it to me. She told me it was an in-depth questionnaire, the clinical standard for measuring if someone has OCD and to what degree. *Aha, I thought. Here we go.*

"Look over it to familiarize yourself with it," she said softly and patiently. "It'll give you a pretty comprehensive list of obsessions and compulsions divided into categories. I'll have you read through every listed example out loud, and you'll verbally answer if you've ever experienced that symptom in the past, even to a low degree, or if you are currently experiencing it."

On the printout was a list of categories that included contamination obsessions, religious obsessions, repeating behaviors, checking compulsions, etc., and examples were given for each category. Next to each example, two boxes were available to check: "Past" and "Present."

"Any questions, Nathan?"

Whenever someone asked me that, I figured it was a sign I should have a question. "Um… not yet!" I was honest.

So, I began my voyage through the questionnaire for the first time. I read aloud what was before me and responded: "'I fear I might harm myself.' No."

She wrote in her notepad.

"'I fear I might harm other people.'" I paused. I felt a small smile coming on and tried to suppress it as if this were a game, and I had already lost. "Yes."

There it was, my first *yes*. I looked up at Dr. Layton, saw her making direct eye contact with me, and said, "Currently." I looked down at the paper and continued.

"'I have violent or horrific images in my mind.' No."

This process went on for another fifteen minutes.

I was relieved by the examples to which I could say, "I've never experienced this," and I felt I was signing an everlasting contract with a devilish entity every time I came across symptoms that did bring me current or past distress.

I didn't relate much to contamination obsessions, which brought me a droplet of relief. When I came across sexual obsessions, specifically, "I have sexual obsessions that involve children or incest," I winced in disgust. Then, I felt bad about my reaction because I remembered that these *unwanted* thoughts plagued real people.

Some other symptoms I responded to in the affirmative were: "I am excessively concerned with morality." I responded, "Yes. Past and present."

"'I have obsessions about symmetry or exactness.'" When the sheet provided an example of handwriting needing to be perfect, I remembered crossing out mistakes on handwritten essays until the error was completely invisible behind an opaque tangle of scratch marks. I replied, "Yes. Past and present."

Moreover, "'I check that I did not harm others.'" I thought about what this meant momentarily. I remembered looking at someone to whom I was just talking to make sure they were okay after I made a simple joke or spur-of-the-moment remark.

I said, "Yes. Present." I moved on. "'I fear saying certain things.'" The examples abounded, especially in terms that were important to me, like *greatness, knowledge*, etc. "Yes. Present."

"'I check that nothing terrible happened.'" Again, "Yes. Present."

Reading through this packet presented a paradigm shift. With every line, I gained new terminology and an under-standing of a potentially disorderly side of myself. I also discovered that Dr. Layton was someone I could talk to about this, making these experiences less secret. Lastly, I was comforted when I realized that someone or some team had to have created this questionnaire and, therefore, saw dozens, if not hundreds, of patients like me. I wasn't alone in feeling like I needed to know or remember certain things—that they wouldn't just remain in my knowledge without conscious reminding or thoughtful recollection. I wasn't the only person out there who checked that I did not harm others.

I responded to the final symptom and delicately handed back the stapled printout, staring at Dr. Layton like a kid trying to hide that they spilled the juice but indicating just that through their expression. I could have benefited from a deep breath, but I was too enraptured in reading her face in anticipation of that carrot being clipped from its string and handed to me.

As I watched her look over her notes, I ruminated about what it might be like to live with some of the more disturbing symptoms I read but didn't exhibit at the time. There should have been an option on the printout for fearing that one would develop obsessive-compulsive symptoms just by reading about them, because that definitely occurred to me.

Dr. Layton looked over her notes for less than a minute before she raised her glasses to rest them on top of her head. She looked at me with her eyes like a placid lake, and with her tone measured, she said, "Well, Nathan, I can tell you this: you definitely have OCD." She took her time, watchful of how this news weighed on me. "Now, I'm not sure how severe it is at this point." A white fog began creeping in between us. "… will take time…" That fog became too thick to hear what she was telling me. While I nodded to what she was saying, that sympathetic piece of me that was wondering what *she* was going through tenaciously resurfaced—I assumed Dr. Layton wanted to make it clear that I was welcome to come back and see her, that I was advised to because she was the best person to treat me despite what little she knew of my symptoms by the end of the appointment. I had nonetheless started chewing like a horse: I caught the carrot. I had OCD. And I still didn't know what this would mean for me.

The final image of the session that is imprinted in my memory is her kind face watching the news soak into me. What I remember next is emerging outside on Broadway, where the frenzy of midtown blitzed my senses. But this time, the sounds fizzled to nothingness when they tried to reach my heart. I was too preoccupied to hear the noise.

I pulled my phone out of my pocket. I searched for my mom's contact information in my recent calls list, but didn't tap her name yet. I continued wandering through town at an easy gait, the most aimless I had ever let myself be in New York since my plane touched down. I took some moments to posture in ways that I thought would enable me to start coming up with ways to tell her what I had just learned about myself. I remembered a quote from Dr. Layton in her voice, "OCD is a chronic disorder. However, it can be treated. If you have this disorder and you embrace the treatment, you stand a good chance of putting your symptoms into remission." In a different posture my body took on, I recalled her saying, "One in forty people have this disorder." I was one in forty.

Then I tapped on my mom's name.

"Hi, Nate! What's up?" I was met with the eager, compassionate voice I had known all my life. I didn't know how to begin, nor did I know how to adjust my plot to the warm greeting. I let some silence hang. "Nate?"

I started by telling her that I had met with a new therapist for the past fifty minutes.

"Oh, that's great, honey!" she exclaimed. Then she asked with her impossibly gentle and soothing voice, "So, how did the session go?"

"Well... apparently, I have OCD."

"Oh." She was surprised, as if someone had popped a balloon next to her. She didn't know what to make of what I told her; our reactions were parallel.

I held the phone to my face as I walked through the neighborhood in my fog. My mother and I were fortunate to share a rock-solid rapport; I could tell she was taken aback, and she didn't know what to make of what I told her. And I knew she could hear my dismay. I pictured her as she listened: somewhat concerned but unsure if this news merited bringing up her sincerest condolences. Though she had worked for decades as a psychotherapist, she worked with addiction and trauma. She was not versed in OCD whatsoever.

"So, what do *you* think about this new... revelation, honey?"

"Well, I have it," I said. I wasn't feeling soft around the edges as I had been my whole life. "There are no two ways around it. And it's chronic."

"Oh. Damn. I'm so sorry, Nate." Her empathy felt like it was stroking my head. She was with me.

"Oh, you know what?" I asked. "Apparently, one in forty people has this disorder. So... you were right, Mom!"

"How do you mean?" she asked, sounding somewhat defensive.

"Like you always said, I'm not your average bear. I'm now statistically not your average bear."

"Oh, sweetheart," she laughed melancholically.

Some silence passed between us. I was the introvert, and my mother was the extrovert in our pair. She picked up the conversation. "I guess all those 'funny stories' from when you were a kid aren't so funny after all, huh?"

"Like what?"

"Like when you slipped in that puddle in front of Nana's house? When you were around three, and you proceeded to tiptoe over that spot for a year whenever you walked over her patch of pavement? Oh… yeah."

"Hm," I almost whispered. The story was totally veracious. I remembered it better now.

"Or even when you were a baby! Oh, my god. I had just taken off your shoes and set them down, and the toe of one was facing one way, and the toe of the other was facing the other way. And you started squirming right out of my arms, so I put you down, and you crawled over to your shoes, and you turned one of the shoes so they both faced the same direction. And then you just crawled right back to me."

"Really? I did that?" I didn't recall this occurrence. My mother had seemingly stowed away these relevant memories in a state of puzzlement, rather than wondering whether mental illness had anything to do with them.

"I thought you were a genius! I thought all of the quirks you exhibited just pointed to your intelligence."

"Huh," I said like a cough. I lost track of my woe over my diagnosis as I was being petted by my mother's funny and tragic stories. I strangely felt good, and deeper down, hopelessly numb.

"Anyway, I wish I had noticed the red flags before you had to find out like this, honey, all on your own."

"It's all right, Mom, I'm okay. I think this isn't going to be… I think this is going to be fine."

"You're welcome to come home if you need to, as long as you know that. You can take a break, have some rest."

"Thank you, Mom, but there's no way I'm doing that."

Her offer was to be expected and utterly absurd. I couldn't just pack up all my things, give up when I was just getting started, and go back to Mom. I was invested in seeing my success story take shape beyond just my headful of hope. New York had popped me in its mouth and begun to chew, but I was not to be spat out.

10
Monarch Migration

It took courage to leave the last step of the staircase that led to the Experimental Theatre Wing and enter into the butterfly migration that occurred there before class every morning.

Many wrote in journals, and many put belongings into or removed them from the lockers and giddily confabulated around this task. Some were dressed in overalls, others in jumpers, joggers, or yoga pants and exercise bras. Women outnumbered the guys here, and trans youth were represented proudly and welcomingly, some transitioning before my eyes over the course of a year. There were lifted chins, hugs reverberating with charged energy. Some were humble. Some were arrogant, but modesty ruled here. All I could think about was how my mood may have appeared as I made my way toward the swinging door that had to be opened to access half of the studio, the door that was impossible to open perfectly. The plank of teal-painted wood embarrassed me because I *always* held it open for a few seconds, just in case anyone was behind me.

When I saw Mark Rylance erupt onto the stage in the Broadway production of *Jerusalem*, he was clearly not combing through mental compulsions and weighing his choices with obsessive attention and doubt. He didn't swivel his head around his shoulder as he made an entrance. My compulsions were my most enormous secret.

Every day, I offered polite and sincere, but ephemeral, smiles to my colleagues when I passed them in the halls every morning. I molded my smile with an artisan's craftsmanship so no one could know I was panicking. If they presumed my quietness meant I was pissed off, my flexible smile surely dissolved those presumptions. I settled to be seen as mysterious, as long I wasn't being cocky. My curved lips were the ferry between my disquiet and some social normality.

When a butterfly swooped in and greeted me, face stretched open, eyebrows dancing, I usually kept the conversation as close to zero as possible and gave the impression that I had somewhere more important to be; the charade I put on was that casual conversation was something that couldn't hold my attention.

I came to learn that many of my ETW cohorts lived with anxiety. They talked about it with their inner circle, like it wasn't unacceptable and toxic. I found out through an original piece shared in a class that one girl even lived with OCD. She told her story of the insurmountable regret she kept with her for years after making a flippant joke about the Holocaust with people she didn't know well. I also understood the painful process behind her years of suffering.

I kept careful tabs on this girl. I intricately kept distance between us both, emotionally and physically. I felt that if I were to ask her about her symptoms, and really listen like I would have, then they could become my symptoms. I also decided that if I were to be vulnerable with her and bond over our shared mental illness, word would spread more quickly than I could control that I was no longer a mysterious and intense artist, but just "the guy with OCD." This was a high-priority threat to my trajectory toward the *general* success that I craved. I wanted to be the next De Niro, a household name, not marginalized to being pointedly affiliated with an idea.

The young lady's and my shared understanding, if ever there was meant to be one, was aborted on my call.

Most students who had anxious episodes plunked into the open arms of their friends when they were going through something. They actually let people read anxiety on their face and took the next step of talking about it. I didn't put the words "my" and "anxiety" together in college, not even in my head. Nobody could know; why should they, when it was something so unworthy? I couldn't imagine acknowledging anxiety in conversation, much less making light of it. Therapy was hard enough—using language to bring into the world experiences I would rather have kept private. I recoiled when my peers treated their anxiety like any hot topic. I had only antagonism for it.

The more I came at my discomforts with hand-sharpened weaponry and a wimpy war cry, the more they pummeled me under their hooves.

Crossing the threshold into the Tisch lounge required lying to myself. I knew this well. The lie was that I was there just to grab an iced chai latte—to get a caffeine boost, as most other college students did in the morning. I was allegedly here to acquire the brown-liquid-containing cup that completed my outfit as a New Yorker.

I actually entered the lounge because it made my jaw chatter in excitement to be around my impassioned contemporaries who studied various artistic disciplines in this building. Students in the Tisch lounge were emotionally charged, chatty, and moved animalistically. They conferred as wolves and gazelles and rabbits did, in a language that felt beyond me. As I ambled into the cacophony, I headed in the general direction of the coffee shop inside. I nearly levitated on my way there.

They threw their limbs around with temper and with grace; guys challenged their friends with testosterone-fueled objections, and girls seemed to lead in the common-sense and spiritually attuned parts of the discussions. I could make out only stray words and uncontextualized sentences, but this was a destination to behold nonetheless; I concluded that all that could be happening in the discussions here was the shaping of the future of theater and these people's identities in the process.

I walked toward my lie, the false object of my desire. I reached the counter of the coffee shop, feeling like I had trudged through a chittering and hooting savanna.

I channeled a muffled version of my excitement in the direction of the barista when I gave my order. Once I told the barista, "That'll be it!" and I paid, the clock started. There was limited time to continue enjoying the plain of creatures at the watering hole. I slowly turned around with one hand over the other in front of my crotch as if I were trying to appear respectful in an incredible museum. At the table next to the shop's pickup counter was a yellow-shirted rascal with his right leg slung over the fat arm of the sofa. Who was I to delineate what was appropriate in a place like this? Maybe in college, lying one's legs over the arm of a sofa wasn't disrespectful; it was a marvelous side effect of having a relaxed and hungry mind.

Once I had my drink, I could no longer loiter in this temple. I had to soak it in.

I looked behind me and had an acrid feeling as I saw the barista adding a few more ice chips to the top of the drink. I looked away and heard him snap on the lid. "Iced chai latte for Nathan?" Time was up.

The air's magic was sucked into an unseen vortex in a corner where the walls and floor met. My lie was in my hand, and now I had to continue pretending that this was all I had come for. The walkway now drew more of my attention than the affable and controversial orbits of conversation. I either had to step up and into one of these circles or get my ass out of there.

My mouth was ajar; I was aching to speak. As I strolled, I looked to my left and saw a guy I knew from ETW in the middle of ebullient lecturing. My heart started thumping like a prompt signal that I should walk over there, and I would be disobeying my body's desire by doing anything but. Yet still, I moved toward the red, four-lettered sign posted above the door. I pictured myself mustering a feeble greeting that no one could even hear, then awkwardly remaining there, saying nothing else, and observing for over thirty seconds. I pictured throwing my arms up in distressed frustration and letting my hands smack my thighs as I stormed away from the circle, finally getting the people's attention, but only by upsetting them.

Over the course of my studies in the Tisch building, I generated more of a rapport with the glowing exit sign above the door than with anyone who made the place worth being in. Back in the lobby, I took another sip from my spiced milk tea, telling myself that the comfort gained from drinking the beverage was the only kind I needed.

11
Hallmark of Mental Health

Before every session, Dr. Layton strode into her waiting room and greeted me discreetly and professionally. Once it was just the two of us inside, she welcomed me with a more enthusiastic candor.

"Hi, Nathan! So? How has your week been?"

"Oh…" I laughed nervously and then turned inward to uncover how to answer the question appropriately. I could have given a greeting without much consideration, but I valued not being flippant or casual. Plus, no one in my environment was asking me how my week was with as much sincerity as Dr. Layton was. It caught me off guard most weeks.

"It's been pretty good." I nodded my head. With each nod, I prepared a response in case she asked me what I meant by "pretty good."

"Yeah? That's good. How have your symptoms been showing up this past week?" she asked with a friendly tone.

I weighed her question. "Yeah, so, well, um... it's been all right." I came to her office every week to express what was getting in my way, yet I was only a few months into learning that I had this disorder in the first place. It wasn't easy to discern what behaviors were unwanted, which thoughts were intrusive, and which experiences were typical. Under Dr. Layton's unshifting gaze, I could sense she wanted me to know I could trust her, but I also felt like she was peeking around and through my verbal offerings, even when I was more articulate. It felt like what I was bringing to the table was falling short of her expectations.

The way I saw it, she was looking for signs of compulsivity behind the facade of my composure. I didn't like feeling examined like this, but she was likely just doing her job well. She nodded after my responses, letting some silence drag before picking the conversation back up as if to say, "Okay, and?" There was some heart of significance I wasn't getting anywhere near. But I was trying.

I was happy to relinquish control to her and her no-bullshit New York attitude whenever she felt it appropriate to take the lead. My fantasy of having the perfect therapist was shattered once she first looked less than thrilled at how I stammered and overthought while putting my symptoms into words. *I can't forget,* I reminded myself: *this woman knows the most about OCD of anyone I've ever met. She is my therapist. Listen up.*

It must have looked like I was waiting for her to speak,

although I was actually trying to decrypt my thoughts and put my experiences into words because she asked, "Are you making friends?"

This question came out of left field, but I could answer this one.

"There are a lot of great people at my studio, really talented people, but I kind of keep some distance between me and them…. I'm not really sure why."

"Maybe that's something we could work on, taking little steps toward introducing yourself and talking to more people at your school!"

I pushed my lips together awkwardly.

"Are you speaking with your parents while you're out here in New York?"

"Oh, um… I think that's another thing I deal with. I feel really strange and, like, uncomfortable making calls to the West Coast. Because, like, it's so far away."

"How do you mean?"

"So, like, since they're so far away, my family really has no way of relating to what I'm going through. And that's just purely because of the thousands of miles between us. So it's like, I don't even know why I would bother."

"Do either of your parents plan to visit you in college? Maybe you would consider bringing one of them with you to therapy for a group session?"

"Huh. I would definitely choose my mom. And… I guess I would consider that!" I found the idea didn't sound so bad.

My mom did spend a week visiting me in Manhattan later that school year and attended one therapy session with

Dr. Layton and me. The most significant episode during the session was when I declared, staring at the carpet between Layton and my mom, "I don't think I respect either of my parents, honestly. Neither of them really provided me with any guidance."

I could feel my mom's heart break when I slandered her parenting style like this, but she quickly internalized her disappointment (I was a lot like her). While other parents may have released incredulous rage at a comment like that, my mother started gently asking questions about the times she remembered providing me guidance in my life. I countered that those efforts were insufficient for my needs.

I had the awareness to critique my mother's and father's parenting style, and with that came a sincere wish. I wished either of my parents had gotten down on one knee when I was a kid and made unflinching eye contact with me as they told me that they believed in me, or told me, "Life is tough, but here's how I deal with the problem you're facing. Nathan? Are you listening to me? I'm only here to help, but you have to look at me. I needed to hear that I could do anything if I put in the work, that life can present challenges, and that there are techniques to manage these challenges.

Both of my parents were dominantly motivated *not* to do the damage their parents did to them. I only learned in high school drama class that trying *not to* do something is far harder than *doing* something—for example, *not* being courageous instead of *being* bashful. To *not convince* instead of *to agree*. So, while my parents devoted nearly all of their energy to creating safe spaces for me, I took the safety they generated for granted and yearned for explicit guidance. My parents' shared oblivion was uncanny. They hardly ever co-parented, yet they both operated with the belief that just by being a-round them (sans explicit guidance), I could learn how to live well.

I was out of line to verbalize my critique in such a harsh way. It was what came out of my mouth because I felt Dr. Layton's office was a safe environment to experiment with what was truthful to me. I didn't get the backlash I expected I would. Both women stayed quite calm, and it was long before Dr. Layton said anything in response to my derogatory assessment of my parents.

Dr. Layton cut into some ruminating I was doing and said, "I just want to be clear with you, okay? So, obsessions are intrusive, unwanted thoughts, right? Sometimes, we call them sticky thoughts." I kept big eyes on her but shifted in my seat anxiously. "When these sticky thoughts intrude, they will usually spark an intensely distressing feeling in someone, like disgust or high anxiety."

I nodded. This sounded all too familiar.

"But these are false thoughts," she said as if that was a delightful encouragement. "I want you to think of these thoughts as *noise* rather than a *signal.* A signaling thought would be a productive or helpful one, like, *I'm hungry,* or *I want to ask that person out.*

"People experience obsessive thoughts all the time. My sister, who does not have OCD, will worry, *Maybe I'll drop the baby.* That's an intrusive thought. But the difference is that

91

she will let it pass. People with OCD don't have the capacity to let the thought pass. They get stuck."

I stayed looking at her, and somewhere from behind my eyes, I felt more ready to verbalize what my symptoms might look like. Her review of what sticky thoughts were infused more personal experiences into my memory. I wondered if she would ask me again about my latest obsessive-compulsive experiences because I was ready.

"I want you to get clear about why you're in treatment for your OCD." This felt like a left turn. "I think this will help you a lot in our work together, to set your intentions about why you want to treat this disorder."

I took a deep breath and sighed as I continued paying attention to her. She pulled a sheet of paper out from a manila folder that was sitting on her desk. She handed me the printout. In a large, colorful, goofy font, the title read, "Why I'm Treating My OCD...."

Underneath the title there were subheadings written in other curly, annoying fonts in loud colors: "I'm doing this for my family," "I want to be free again," "I deserve to be happy," "I'm taking my life back," and, "OCD will not rule me." As I held this sheet in my hands, the phrases printed on it arrived to me as if a wanderer mumbled them to me from across a desert. They were nice sentiments, but I could tell they wouldn't do me any good. I still smiled and evoked a convincing gratitude for Dr. Layton's gesture. I said nothing about how unnecessarily bouncy the font was as I carefully slid the handout into my backpack.

"Again, this will help you set your intentions about why you're treating this disorder. It's so important to keep in mind what you're doing this *for*."

I couldn't take what she said seriously, as significant as she made it seem.

"Before you leave today," she resumed, "I want to leave you with something, Nathan. I tell this to all my patients, and it's the essence of our work together. So, what I want you to remember is this: flexibility is the hallmark of mental health."

Whoa. I wasn't prepared for a remark that boomed like a cannon and was so sage. Was I flexible? Were we really dealing with my comprehensive "mental health" here, not just OCD? I certainly wasn't great at adapting to unexpected situations, if that's what she meant by flexibility.

"We're coming up to that time," she said with a smile. I watched her face painstakingly—was she satisfied with the appointment? Was she disappointed in me? Was she just ready to see her next patient?

She wrote down some homework for me as she did at the end of every session and handed me the half-sheet of lined notebook paper. It detailed tasks for me to fulfill that were in the trajectory of our therapeutic work. She let me read it, told me not to forget to do it, and walked me to her door.

"I'll see you next week!"

As I walked home, I mulled over that phrase: *flexibility is the hallmark of mental health.* I worked on forming an image for the word "hallmark." It was a word I didn't come across often, except when I saw the name of the greeting card company and the television network.

I pictured a gleaming, golden arch like half of the McDonald's logo with wide bases and a thinner pinnacle. I pictured myself reaching toward the top of the arch. The funny thing was that the pinnacle was not very far from the base. I felt like I had reason to celebrate because my hallmark was attainable.

12
Homework

I arrived back at my dorm and greeted what awaited me: the subject of tonight's homework, my desk. I read the scrawling on the half-sheet of lined notebook paper I still had in my pocket.

It read.

Clean up desk, allowing yourself to do it imperfectly.

Step on at least one leaf and at least two grates when you want to avoid stepping on them.

Embrace that you can have a bad day in class. Meanwhile, resist turning head.

The items proceeded along what was called a "hierarchy" of increasingly challenging tasks for me to complete over the week between sessions. *Clean up desk, allowing yourself to do it imperfectly,* I reread. I looked at my messy desk. It had all sorts of arbitrary items strewn over it and even some pieces of trash. I had been avoiding tidying it up because I dearly feared there was no *perfect* way to do it. I feared the consequences of failing to clean it well were too close to matters of the heart. If I over-altered the appearance of the desk by moving objects and harming the space, then I would fail in building quality social relationships, and I would not learn anything in my classes. The assignment from Dr. Layton, of course, was to accept these consequences and give it a try.

I neglected my homework assignments in high school. I hated being told what to read and how many chapters in a book to complete by a certain date. I read only two or three of the dozen-plus books assigned for at-home reading in high school. I felt strongly that institutions of learning and therapy should be capable of accomplishing all of their goals for me without loading me up with surplus work to do at the location where I intended to relax.

I sat down on my bed and woefully stared at my desk full of trinkets, papers, and plastic wrappers. I looked down at the sheet of four or so homework assignments from my therapist. I folded it back up and tried to commit to memory what she wrote on the sheet of paper. I had myself sure that I was taking to heart what she was asking of me. As I went about my day, I *imagined* what it would feel like to soak myself in my particularly repetitive fears and resist engaging in the corresponding compulsion. I treated the assignment much like an acting exercise. I made the "imagination" step of the assignment engorged with significance. I figured if I could *imagine* the pain of resisting a compulsion by accepting the threats of one of my unwanted thoughts, then I could rightfully call it a day and be able to say I finished the homework.

I flexed my acting muscles when she asked me about the previous week's homework. I inhaled a vibrant interest in her question and replied, "I feel like the homework went really well over the week!" She rarely challenged a positive sentiment to test whether it was true. I knew I was doing the bare minimum of those tasks she asked me to do during my own time. I learned I could just purposefully confuse doing the *least* with doing my *best*.

She was an intelligent woman; she knew the value of the present moment over reports from the past in our limited fifty minutes together. Moving on was more valuable to her than examining the previous week.

As soon as I learned that Dr. Layton had no real way of tracking my fulfillment of the homework, that she couldn't judge me for doing very little anyway, and she was here to serve me in any state I was in, I wove pride into the delusion that I put effort into the homework.

"Yeah! I stepped on a few leaves and grates today that I would have preferred to avoid. That was good. I felt a lot of anxiety when I crunched on the leaf, but I guess that's the point, isn't it? So, yeah, I feel pretty good about what I did." It was all made up.

It was already hard work nurturing OCD. Breaking down the internal structures it boasted was not the kind of work that interested me. The majority of at-home therapeutic tasks requested of me felt like an outrage to my ability to decide how to use my time. There was no one who could tell me a better way to use my time than I could.

When I spoke to Dr. Layton, I saw her not only as a supportive resource but also as an example of behavior and a mind that were not obsessive-compulsive. I confided in her during a session that I wanted to trust myself. I said it with naive adoration for the idea. She responded immediately with, "You can't trust yourself, Nathan. You have OCD. You can't *trust* your thoughts."

She offered further context about what she meant, but the sharpness with which she instinctively responded had already struck me, and it felt like it broke the skin.

I can't trust myself?

This was preposterous for one reason: Ralph Waldo Emerson was my favorite giant of literary history. I didn't read all his work, but I was, unfortunately, more loyal to the long-dead philosopher-writer than to Dr. Layton. One of his core tenets was that the genius's way was total self-trust.

As the session proceeded, I was thinking, *She must mean that she doesn't want me to get carried away. I have no choice but to trust myself. I am an individual.*

I understood why Dr. Layton let out her urgent and less-than-tactful response. She didn't want me trusting the wrong thoughts. Dr. Layton never found out how much I valued self-trust. But perhaps she read it on my face as I performatively thought in her office, sending her down misleading paths with many pregnant silences. I didn't like being figured out. I didn't want to control Layton's mind either; I enjoyed being in awe at her knowledge and neurotypical presence. When it came to relaying my internal experiences, I struggled because I had more faith in transcendental thinkers (who preached self-reliance) than any lesser-known therapist with whom I had a direct relationship. Self-trust was the only viable lifestyle I could see granting me happiness.

13
Romance-adjacent

I've always felt nervous about interrupting groups of girls to talk to them. And this is almost always required to talk to girls. No one likes being interrupted, but maybe girls know to expect it if they want to be swept off their feet (or however that works)

I came to college a virgin, considering sex an encounter with scripted inevitability. I associated sex with relentless physicality from the man, and absurd, performative pleasure from the woman. I was sickly addicted to pornography. I was hooked to the carnival of ecstasy that was a couple of search terms away at any time.

When I came to college, I thought my type was poised, sensitive, and kind girls. If they didn't check these three boxes, they were not for me. But a few months into the traveling circus of rooftop parties hosted by upperclassmen that all ETW students were invited to every other week, the rules changed. I was falling for the painfully shy girl. I had feelings for the overly awkward girl. I liked spiritual girls. I liked goth girls. I liked selfish girls. I liked selfless girls. I liked all the girls.

But I treasured being friends with intriguing women more than anything. I unconsciously and accurately gauged that I needed a woman's friendship more than anything else to evolve in the ways I needed to: by becoming grounded in a healthy relationship and growing in the direction of trust.

Emily became my friend through a series of subtle events. We looked at each other when someone made a joke, or we intuitively sought each other out in mundane ways, like meeting for lunch at a dining hall or helping each other with our homework assignments. We worked together collaboratively in class, and we found ourselves eventually having the other over to our dorm for dinner with our roommates or other mutual acquaintances. She could have been an immense resource if I had ever asked for any help. She was the most selfless being I had ever met.

When I imagined myself asking a girl like Emily out, I saw a scene of me looking at my feet, pulling nervously at my sleeves, looking away from her, not knowing where to propose we go.

When another girl who studied at ETW confided in me, "I always thought you and Emily would end up together!" I raised my eyebrows at her comment and instinctively replied, "Me too!"

That put a strange button on that conversation. I could have asked Emily out, but I never did.

Dr. Layton clued me in during a session: "OCD gets worse under a few circumstances: when you're really tired, when you're alone, when you drink, when you're stressed, and when you're doing something you truly love, unfortunately. OCD will eventually latch on to the things you care about most."

Asking a girl out felt intolerable as a fantasy, yet I further imagined what being on a date would be like. That is where the unwanted thoughts proliferated: *Maybe I'll walk into the restaurant with my mouth gaping open, letting out a guttural scream. I could spill coffee on myself while I'm weaving a story and need to leave to tend to my singed groin. Maybe I'll be so distracted with anticipating and dreading our lunch out that I won't shower before, and she'll only be able to manage false smiles as she tries to quell her disgust at my stench.*

I was a straight white male in a female-dominated theater program. I understood that I was one of the most eligible bachelors in my environment. Yet I didn't sense that I was possessed with the power to successfully court women. That was something other guys did. I was responsible for deciding how to conduct myself and shaping an identity that was distinct from my actions, so how could I assemble all my faculties and implement them toward trying to get a woman into bed? It made no sense and sounded impossible.

I didn't have the experience required to think with my penis. Maybe if it had gotten any action in high school (or middle school, for that matter), then I would have been more adept at organizing casual physical encounters with women.

I wanted to believe modern cultural premises like "F*ck b*tches, get money," "These hoes ain't loyal," "Girls aren't worth your energy, bro" and "She just wants attention." But in them, I heard little but male manipulation and making women out to be weak when they weren't.

Among the options for successfully interrupting groups of girls were to be bright-eyed and bushy-tailed and act like a friend, or I could be more of an instrument of romance and seek to seduce one or more of the women there through my actions and conversational output. What I ended up doing most of the time was embodying an altogether inclusive flirtatiousness. It consisted of strategic eye contact, controlled smirks, and letting my aura lead the way. I hoped my interest in the women around me radiated from me as intensely as I felt it did.

I ventured past letting my aura do the talking when I went to ETW parties. On the receiving end of generous pours of rum and Coke with the occasional edible in hand, I enjoyed learning from the panoply of behaviors perceivable at parties. All the action was in the gushing and flowing faces of the partygoers. I participated in impromptu photoshoots with DSLR cameras, the flash on, and our drama at a high. Or I shared a joint with a circle of brilliant artists as we gossiped about our professors, all of us impersonating a few of them. At one party, the hostess emerged from her apartment bedroom completely nude and spent the rest of the evening without clothing on, inviting her friends and cohorts to make whatever they would of what they saw. The rooftops where ETW parties happened were perfectly suited to the absolute limitlessness of the evening's scope. I reached for infinity with one hand and held onto a Solo cup with the other. Young geniuses surrounded me; yet even better, they were accessible.

At these parties, eye contact puzzled and frustrated me. I studied the moist, spherical organs of my peers, watching the aperture of their irises and pupils change, hoping to learn something about what made eye contact valuable. But in my white-knuckling, I missed the delicate lessons that eye contact provides only when one listens. Only when I wasn't looking for the power of eyeballs did I sense the power of eyes. But often, I was so determined to see something worth writing home about, I missed the gems one only catches by letting go.

Beyond finding my study of eye contact tragically inert, I felt all of my identity was threatened the longer I kept my eyes on another person. Because I could estimate other people's personalities, it meant mine was on the market to be taken and never returned.

I was jarred with paranoia that all the qualities I liked about myself were at risk whenever I was paying attention to someone. While sitting on the host's bed with an upper-classman girl and three other people in the room, I listened to them discuss the children's book by comedian Bo Burnham and eventually gush over his status as a comic phenom. I nodded pretty ferociously and wore a pleased smile, but participating in this conversation meant that I could lose my ability to assess what good comedy was. I cared more about preserving my taste than risking it for passing conversation.

I was embraced at these parties by brilliant and humble folks, lovingly so. Still, the encouragements and invitations they hurled toward me may as well have had the power of torpedoes, coming to destroy everything I knew about myself. If I had a conversation where I fell too deeply into the other person, I would lose track of myself and never regain it.

Because I couldn't stand the idea of losing myself, I was cautious.

I never even considered this could be a symptom of a disorder, nor that this was a struggle that likely nobody else at the party suffered from.

As I chatted with Emily on our way back from a soirée, I ducked my head before smiling at what she was saying. I looked beyond her as she spoke, as if something had caught my eye, but I was really waiting for a safe moment to return to genuine eye contact. I used eye contact not as a tool to build trust but only wielded it periodically to let her know I loved that she was there.

14
Imran

Another person who stopped me in my tracks in the ETW halls and insisted on opening me up so we could be friends was Electric. Electric had electrons rapidly whizzing around her at all times, making her socially facile and highly sensitive. She connected with people more formidably than I'd ever seen and forged connections between her friends who were strangers to each other like I'd never known.

Once she decided I was cool—or maybe it was that I was promising enough to belong under her wing—she wanted to share the wonders that lay within one of her neighbors with me. As we trotted down the hall of her dormitory to introduce me to her floormate, Imran, she hurriedly said, "I just know you'll love this guy. He's super crazy." She snickered as she continued, "But he's also really fucking smart."

Once Electric opened the door, the overwhelming scent signified to all of us that the vital task was getting in and shutting the door behind us as quickly as possible so the marijuana smoke wouldn't waft down the hall to the RA's room. It was night, and few lights were on in Imran's room. As I passed into the atrium, I understood why. His view of the city was astonishing. Imran was an unassuming silhouette with gawky limbs that swung awkwardly. As I walked in closer, he became an eager young man who wore a huge, attractive grin that made me wonder what having such nice teeth was like.

With his blown-glass pipe in hand, he welcomed us enthusiastically, eyeing the smoke seeping through the doorway. "Hurry up! Come on in!"

I entered his space and felt that thunderclap of knowing there was no returning the same.

"Hi, man! I'm Imran!" He had a speech impediment I didn't know to expect.

"Imran? Hi, I'm Nathan! It's good to finally meet you."

The small talk was evanescent, luckily. Imran giddily caught up with Electric and, without words, encouraged me to make myself at home with the ease he had in his own skin. It immediately became evident that Imran cared as little about the hideous task of exchanging pleasantries as I did.

"Yeah, so," he started saying, "My name is like 'him' without the 'H—'" he paused, waiting for me.

"Okay. Im."

"And 'Ron,' like 'Ron Swanson.' Imran!"

"All right. Imran. Got it!" I confirmed, amused by his candor.

Most of the people I met at NYU were actors, and actors' faces were highly legible most of the time. Imran was no actor. He studied computer science, based on what Electric told me before I met him. I was dismayed to see that my peers often hid their true selves under painfully obvious layers of effort and strategy. I knew what they were sharing wasn't the whole enchilada, yet I was rarely willing to continue exploring if that person was going to reveal themselves more authentically down the road. As far as my style, I liked to think I was not so much a masker but an abstainer who remained in an acute state of listening.

Imran didn't seem to participate in freelance self-concealing like all the other young strategists at NYU did. He was humorously authentic.

He hit his pipe a few more times and carried on with Electric, picking up wherever they had left off since they last saw each other. I watched the curly tufts of black hair that extended more than a couple of inches above his head bounce as he chuckled heartily. The joy of his giggles transferred to me.

"So, you're an actor like Electric? And you also go to ETW?" he asked as if the coincidence were a miracle on earth.

"That's right! You got it. Wow, I've been introduced already." I looked at Electric and smiled shyly at her, impressed by what he knew about me.

I was disappointed that I couldn't make out all his words; some of his language sounded like it came out of his nasal passage, muddled. I assumed his intermittent spoken incomprehensibility had something to do with the wide and flat scar tissue above his upper lip. I tried to hide the fact that I noticed the facial scar tissue, but simultaneously, I was humbled when I realized maybe Imran knew suffering as I did.

"So, get this. Imran's from—well, tell him where you're from, Ronnie."

"Oh, yeah, sorry." He shook his head as if he had forgotten to tell us he had won the lottery that morning. "I'm from a tiny island called Mauritius," he told me, revealing his place of origin like he was weaving his favorite tale. "It's off the coast of Africa, next to Madagascar."

"Okay… Mauritius." I thought about his country's name. I was a longtime geography nerd who played for a hundred hours or more with a talking globe that was gifted to me by my grandfather. Still, this country hardly rang a bell. "Sounds sort of familiar. I definitely know where Madagascar is." He was delighted by this. Then I explained that I knew about the country of Madagascar before the animated movie of the same name. He derived even more pleasure when I shared this.

"It is a paradise island, bro. Let me tell you, ohhhhh, my gosh."

"Wow...." The reality of this hit me: "You're from Africa! That is so cool, man." Imran's lack of artifice hooked my attention. "So, when was your first time in America?" I asked.

"This is my first time!" He nodded feverishly.

"Seriously?! Well, I never would have guessed it. You seem super comfortable, man."

"Thank you, thank you. Oh, and I don't know if I mentioned it, but my roommate had a nervous breakdown basically at the beginning of the year and left after two weeks. So, I have the place to myself, and we can smoke whenever we want! Shall we?"

I grinned at his offer. We all crouched in his plain bathroom with a towel stuffed under the door and got high together. As we passed the paraphernalia with care and respect, trust started blossoming between us.

I told him that my father had gone on a solo trip to Kenya and Rwanda in the early 2000s. This was my sincerest effort to show my fascination with the distance Imran had traveled to study in New York City. I had to ask him to repeat himself multiple times, yet he glided over the matter for a couple of hours. As we emerged from the bathroom, he clarified why I was having some difficulty understanding all his words: "When I get really high, I forget to pronounciate? Pronunciate? My words carefully. I was born with what's called a double cleft lip," (he ran a finger over his scar) "and a cleft —"

"Oh my gosh," I let out sympathetically.

"—palate."

I had seen one journalistic television program on this challenging facial deformity, and from what little I learned about it, living with it was not for the faint of heart. Imran was proof.

"Yeah, bro," he continued. "I had to have nine invasive surgeries from the time I was born until I turned nineteen."

"Holy shit, man."

"And, every time I had a surgery, like, I had to teach myself to talk and walk again. Because the doctors borrowed bone from my hip to put in my face."

"Wow. You're a warrior, dude."

"Oh yes," he laughed. "And thank you." He looked relieved that I hadn't chosen to tell him how sorry I was.

Imran's honesty reminded me of no one I knew, but it made me feel at home. When he made eye contact, there was no haughty blaze behind his eyes that told me he was aching to be the alpha. In fact, Imran rarely made eye contact when he spoke. He sort of got lost in weaving his stories and forming his ideas, perhaps searching for words that were best expressed in his mother tongue of French. I detected a little vanity, but considering all his other favorable qualities, it was complementary to him.

Imran was studying computer science at the College of Arts and Sciences. He was the first computer science major I had spent any time with at NYU. I comprehended how far Imran was from an actor or dancer; he carried his body erratically, like a six-year-old in swimming lessons. He explained, however, that Tisch students were the Americans he preferred to keep in his closest circles.

"I just love Tischies, bro," he said. "They're all such interesting people. They take me to musicals and do what they truly love, even though there's no real money in it. I really admire that."

He was being sincere, but this made me laugh.

"I've been thinking about getting into producing theater," he continued.

Electric was blending into the walls, which was typically impossible for her to do. Maybe she was dampening her zaniness to give us a chance to bond.

There was something else I couldn't put my finger on that drew me to Imran like a soft campfire at night. I didn't have the words myself; then, Imran just happened to unveil this trait as he continued talking about his goal of producing theater: "... I'm very emotionally intelligent," he announced, with varying inflection and the lightest suggestion of a smile.

Imran was the kind of guy who could spin a tale (especially about himself) for ages. In the span of one night, I learned that Imran was a self-taught computer programming virtuoso. He was open enough to share with me that his father died when he was young, and as he described, "The computer was my only friend. So, I wanted to learn the language it had to teach me." He taught himself to code.

As he went on, he labeled himself, paired with his approachable, beaming grin: "I'm a prodigy, not quite a genius." I laughed at his ridiculous, though probably veracious, self-classification.

I was curious if he was born with charisma and high self-esteem or had to fight to develop these traits to come out on top of his health-related battles. I had the sense, for some reason, that his winning personality was hard-won.

Electric bid us adieu and trotted back down the hall to bed. Imran and I both wanted to keep propelling the evening, and we agreed to venture into Times Square. We gave each other looks standing in the aisle of the subway car that communicated, "You can't possibly be as smart as you sound, right? No, you definitely are. Please, go on." If one were to strip away our primary interests and histories, we were two very similar people.

We chose a burger joint smack-dab in Times Square for dinner. Under the unnecessarily effulgent lights of the restaurant, I got to soak in the gratitude for finding my first male friendship in college that developed serendipitously and speedily as I decided the best ones did.

After meeting Imran, the passing of my time wasn't marked only by rituals that created a stuttering sequence of days. I felt more empowered to allow my compulsivity to fade in its rigor when I hung out with Imran, Wyatt, Moriah, and Emily. The curtain was about to close on my first school year at NYU.

Imran and I decided to room together for our sophomore year. We said "yes" without any coddling of egos or feigned disinterest. I loved this guy. Our journey as brothers was only beginning.

15

The Uncertainty Archway

During the next session, several months into our work together, Dr. Layton quickly took the conversation's trajectory into her own hands. "Okay," she began, "I want to take some time to educate you and go into detail about the kind of therapy we're doing together here."

I leaned forward. This sounded like it was going to be good.

"So, the work we're doing is technically categorized as CBT, cognitive behavioral therapy. I think we've talked about CBT, have we?"

"Yeah, we have. I think you mentioned it in the first session, actually."

"Great! Okay, so what CBT is all about is that we're intervening at the behavioral level. It's very hard to change one's thoughts or feelings with our will, but shifting our behavior is possible. Our specific work is a branch of CBT that's called ERP: exposure and response prevention. ERP is the best treatment approach we have ever had for OCD. By we, I mean the medical community.

"It consists of welcoming or *exposing* yourself to your distressing thought that is unwanted, seeking it out instead of pushing it away. Then we're *preventing* the response to the thought, which is the compulsive behavior, by resisting following up with your habituated behavior. If your thought tells you, 'I'm a pedophile,' or 'I will contract AIDS,' I want you to just say, 'I don't know, I might be a pedophile. So be it.' Just say, 'I don't know if I'll get AIDS. We'll see.'

"The more you argue with OCD, the stronger it gets. OCD cannot be reasoned with. It's an irrational disorder. It's a terrible, cruel disorder, it really is." She echoed this sentiment from a previous session. It was one she felt deeply.

I felt quite calm in her presentation of this material. I could tell she had a firm grasp of the content she was illustrating for me. I had my ears open and was interested in what the real treatment plan was all about. I wanted to untangle my head from the knots that OCD had tangled me in. I appreciated that she understood OCD as something separate from *me*. She talked about it like an outside force I could face head-on instead of a part of my brain I somehow had to change without neurosurgery.

She went on, "The goal here is to actually *trigger* yourself by approaching a situation that provokes your anxiety or makes you feel unsure. Seeking out anything that may spark a thought that you don't want to have. The thing is, they're just thoughts. Many people have intrusive thoughts, and they let them go. People have these thoughts all the time. But it's very difficult for people with OCD to let an unwanted thought go. They hold onto it and argue with it, seeking absolute certainty that the thought can't come true. This fighting with your thoughts just makes the urge to ritualize stronger."

She could clearly carry on for hours on the topic. I was eating up her description, so grateful for her willingness to go into detail, even though I imagined she did this same spiel for hundreds of other patients. I was probably one of her quieter patients, though, so she likely got to expand on the subject of our work more than she usually could.

She continued, "And the medication is known to help you with this work, to make it easier to face."

I started taking Prozac two months into our work, at Dr. Layton's recommendation. She told me that the medication would make the exposure and response prevention work easier to face. As I assessed its effects on me in real time, I noticed I was creating projects in class with more fluidity, but I felt more analytical and logical. I felt estranged from the creative instinct that makes the whole artistic process worthwhile.

Still, I continued trusting Dr. Layton's recommendation that the use of an SSRI drug (serotonin-specific reuptake inhibitor) like Prozac would be beneficial to my healing.

Dr. Layton summarized the topic of the day by asking, "So, if the unwanted thought tells you, 'Class is going to be a disaster,' you say…"

"I'm screwed. And… that's okay?"

She chuckled. "You say, 'I don't know if class will be a disaster, bring it on!' Right? You don't fight with the thought. Embracing the premise of our unwanted thoughts will make it easier to block your desire to engage in the compulsion, the response. That's why we've been working on identifying what your compulsions are, because it seems you have more compulsions than obsessions, whereas some people have more obsessions and mental compulsions than physical compulsions. This is also why I have you on medication. The medication makes it a lot easier for you to resist doing the rituals. It basically circulates the serotonin that is normally lacking in the brains of people with OCD. Okay?"

She looked at me like she was watching a young child enjoy candy. I wasn't that thrilled, but I almost got lost in her gaze. The fifty minutes I got with her each week were a prized possession of mine, a resource to avert me from the inane directives of OCD.

"I know this will be tough. OCD is tough. But you can beat it. I know you can. The more you say 'I don't know' and approach uncertainty, the better off you'll be."

"All right." I smiled. *Approach uncertainty? What the hell does that even mean?* I wondered. I didn't want to seem dumb, so I kept the question to myself. "Okay. I see. But what if I can't identify what the obsessive thought is, or if I don't have a thought around a particular compulsion?"

"In that case, you should have a sense of what your triggering circumstances are. It might be being in a certain place, touching a certain thing, or talking with a certain person. These kinds of things can activate anxiety and make you want to protect yourself by engaging in rituals."

Her general examples of triggering circumstances gave way to boundless, more detailed examples of the triggers that came to mind: Whenever I was near the gaping parking garage at Broadway and Astor Place, the mouth of the garage demanded a few dedicated seconds of my attention for me to be able to advance. There was touching the swinging door in ETW, and talking with fellow artists about... well, most anything.

"Okay, that makes sense." I was getting a little anxious now, just imagining the concept of intentionally resisting a compulsion entirely. I orchestrated all of my rituals to repel the skin-crawling anxiety that always preceded these behaviors. Now, I had to do the reverse.

"Now. If you can't prevent yourself from doing your compulsion that time, it is still a win in my book if you can *delay* it. Delaying the response is an achievement because you'll start to feel what it's like to proceed through your life without engaging in a ritual as soon as you get the urge to do so. The more space we introduce between the trigger and the response, the better off you'll be.

"The main thrust of our work is *approaching uncertainty*. All OCD is designed to push away uncertainty at any cost. Just deny its existence. 'I don't want anything to do with it.' That's why OCD will have you engaging in repetitive behaviors again and again because you can't feel absolutely certain that you got your protective habit right and got completely rid of that unsettling thought. 'Did I get AIDS when I cut my finger?' Most people, if that thought occurs to them, would just let it pass, but the uncertainty is something people with

OCD typically can't tolerate. So that's one key thing that we're doing here: we want to *approach* uncertainty, Nathan."

I squinted as though I didn't understand.

She looked back, somewhat concerned, with a wrinkle in her brow that wasn't there before. I tried not to look too confused. I wanted to come across as intelligent to my therapist so she would think well of me. On several occasions, I imagined what it would be like if she had OCD, introducing these topics with much more hesitancy and gentleness, and even ritualizing herself. She couldn't be farther from it. She had peeled back the skin and looked into the belly of the beast several years ago and selected a life where she helped people subtract all power from that beast.

"When you say uncertainty," I finally remarked, taking my time, "it feels like you're talking about nothing. Like there's nothing *there* to approach when I hear that."

"Right, but there is," she said with a big smile. "Uncertainty is… everywhere. It's everything we don't know. And everybody, everybody deals with it. Not just people with OCD. You have a disorder that prevents you from being okay with this enormous force in life, and that's one huge reason for us to be doing this work." She sat back and got more comfortable in her chair. If I had more questions, she was clearly ready. This was her domain.

My attention was invested in her. I soaked up as much as I could of what she was saying. And I didn't like the sound of any of it.

"The more you go toward uncertainty, the more you are disarming OCD." She picked up the torch. "You're taking away its authority to say, 'You're not doing this right,

Nathan,' or 'You will harm that person, Nathan.' There's no way to know! There's no way to know. And that's what I want you to be okay with. And we'll start small with responses you'll have an easier time doing away with. But we're welcoming the not knowing."

I gave her a blank stare. Then I looked out the window. I could have used some fresh air.

"And I know this'll be tough. I know." More silence hung between us. "But believe me, when you start inviting your intrusive thoughts instead of batting them away, and when you welcome uncertainty step by step, you'll start seeing what's possible for you."

"Right. But..." I forced myself to say it, at the risk of sounding dumb: "What is uncertainty? Like... if I can't identify it, how will I know how to 'approach' it? Like, if I can't see it or anything?"

She leaned forward with her rimless glasses framing her eyes. "You'll sense it, Nathan. The more practice you give yourself, the more you'll start *feeling* what it is. You've been trained by OCD to stay far away from uncertainty, so you may not recognize it right away, and you'll want to turn away when you do sense it." She seemed like she was having fun. "But we want to instead go toward it, whatever it is. Go toward what you don't know.

"I'm going to give you an assignment to take on a compulsion that you feel you would have a somewhat easier time removing from your life. Something other than the looking behind you, which we've been working on. You can think of one now. Take your time."

I squirmed in my seat and looked down.

Dr. Layton was chipping away at the tangled heart of my disorder, beginning to challenge all of its cruel defense systems. If what she was saying was true, and I truly did believe her, my OCD defenses were *penetrable*. And what felt wonderful to hear was that this wasn't my fault. She spoke of OCD as if it were a secondary, outside player, a villain that I was involved with, not an unfortunate part of my own brain. And though that felt like such a typical therapeutic technique, I didn't care. Because it also felt empowering. *Maybe I can beat this thing*, she inspired me to think. Approaching uncertainty was the boldest invitation I had ever been given in my life, so I took it one week at a time.

She knew how terrible OCD was from seeing it ravage people's lives, but she could never really feel its power on a constant, moment-to-moment basis. With this awareness, I could honor that I knew my symptoms better than anyone, while she knew how to get me away from their clutches better than anyone. The relationship was working for me… at this moment. Walking away from the session to take on the homework of facing this new compulsion all on my own would be an entirely different challenge.

I didn't enjoy the prospect of approaching what felt like a bodiless, airy suggestion of a thing she called uncertainty. I still, at this point, felt that it was simply nonexistent. I could tell welcoming this transient force into my life would be unnerving. All my habits were in place to repel uncertainty, to vanquish it, and now she wanted me to sit with it and peer into its eyes lovingly. *I'm not sure if I can stomach it.* I had my work cut out for me.

"I think I know one habit I can start with. It would be, like, purposefully stepping on leaves and cracks in the sidewalk because I definitely avoid them right now."

"And why do you think you're stepping around those things when you see them now? What do you think might happen if you step on a leaf or a line in the sidewalk?"

"I'm not sure. Maybe I'm afraid that something bad will happen or I'll be completely unprepared for class."

"Great. Perfect."

"Oh, and sewer grates. I guess I can try to step on those too." My panic was already rising, thinking about shifting my walking habits to include these previously untouchable features of any sidewalk.

"Great! So, walk me through what this will look like, Nathan."

"So, okay. So if I see a leaf that I don't want to step on, I say, 'My day might be a disaster,' and I just step on it?"

"Exactly. Excellent. Just live with the anxiety. Just sit with it. Let it pass over you, and watch it as it does."

"And approach... uncertainty."

"Yes. If you find you can live with the anxiety that comes up, terrific. If you find that this exposure is too difficult and the anxiety is overcoming you in a way that's too much for you, then so be it. You can try not stepping on a sewer grate. But watch what happens to your anxiety as you do that. The more you ritualize, the deeper your anxiety will actually go."

"Hm. Okay." *They're just leaves,* I tried telling myself when I knew they were determinants of the rest of my day. *Uncertainty. Uncertainty,* I said to myself.

She handed me the sheet of homework.

After I left her office, I repeated to myself what I deemed her seminal phrase: *Flexibility is the hallmark of mental health.* I envisioned what true flexibility might look like and pictured a hand trying to stand up a cooked noodle, and the noodle flopping over every time.

I thought about what uncertainty could be. I imagined a hundred-foot-tall, cloudy, gray archway planted a half-mile down the street from me. If I were to ever find this arch and pass under it, then I would somehow understand myself better on the other side. That's what I grasped. I was underground, but slowly and surely digging toward the light. Dr. Layton was there to help me dig in the right direction.

16
Galaxy of Profundity

When I returned to Gramercy Green, I greeted my buddy Imran and automatically agreed to enter the bathroom to smoke. For him, skipping to the loo could have been out of pleasure. For me, it was out of habit. After years of use, the act of picking up the bong, lighting the weed, and inhaling became a compulsive act in itself. I was in denial of this fact, but the signs were present: I felt anxious and bored, so I reached for weed. After I smoked, I spent two hours dancing with heightened paranoia mixed with a delicious release from my psyche's fist. I released into all of myself, my self-predatory thoughts, and my scrumptiously charged creativity alike.

Since high school, my buddies and I hardly ever took our time when smoking. We hardly ever sipped at the lip of the bong or the blunt. We chugged the tea. Maybe our smoking was powerfully mechanical because we were unwitting addicts of some of the strongest cannabis to be found anywhere.

When I smoked weed, I felt inspired. I stepped into a visceral expansion of my thought types. New modes of thinking were possible in this state. I created rabidly, freestyle rapping in the middle of Manhattan's midnight. When an obsessive thought inevitably wormed its way into my euphoric headspace like a phantom insect, it was scary, and I trusted it. I responded to the danger with prompt mental compulsive behavior. In the swirl of innovation and terror, I was sooner motivated to avoid having a bad high than I was to carry out the therapeutic exposure and response prevention work while high.

Why did I bother with marijuana at all?

I smoked routinely because when I encountered bursts of anxiety while high, they were colorful. It stroked my face, swaths of deep violet, warm crimson, and bright orange. I so looked forward to forging into the psychoactive frontier that I overlooked the paranoid thoughts about the likelihood that I was having a heart attack, and that something I didn't say five minutes prior would profoundly poison my friends' lifetime trajectories if I didn't say something now.

I loved learning while high. Every time I smoked marijuana, once again I had the meta power to decide what "being high" meant.

I fell into a pattern of smoking every day because nights were not as fun when I wasn't stoned.

Wyatt brought it up casually as he was pouring himself a drink in his dorm: "Hey man, would you be down to try LSD?"

I had heard the three stories of each time Wyatt took LSD. The substance had a tremendous impact on him, and yet he was befuddled when he tried to put his experiences into words. I'd never considered taking psychedelics, just like I never considered bottle-feeding a baby pig. I wasn't against it; I just hadn't been presented with the opportunity until now.

"Damn…" I thought of how LSD had changed Steve Jobs' life. I thought of Jimi Hendrix and Eric Clapton. If LSD so famously expanded the minds of these timeless and lauded musicians, I potentially had plenty to gain. I had little to lose. "You know what?" I responded, "I'm down. When do you want to do it?"

The plans changed after Wyatt's proposition. Both Imran and I took LSD for the first time. It was a spring day late in my sophomore year when Wyatt arrived at our Gramercy Green dorm room with four tabs of acid: two for me and two for Imran. Wyatt generously agreed to be our designated "trip sitter." Wyatt wished he could have hallucinated through a journey with us. Instead, he made the responsible decision to smoke a few massive blunts alongside us to get as near as he could to psychedelia while still being able to step in adeptly if we needed guidance.

Imran and I put the two tabs of acid under our tongues at the same time per Wyatt's instructions.

Imran announced his anticipation for his psychedelic journey, "Dude, I can't wait for this. I'm going to be like

Deadpool. I'm not going to give a fuck about anything."
Wyatt and I glanced at each other after this comment. Imran
must not have picked up on the clues Wyatt gave us that this
was a profoundly powerful substance that might impact
Imran deeper than stylizing him as a comic book character.

Forty minutes after the tabs had dissolved, I started
reaching over my head with one arm and stretching my legs.
I figured gentle yoga was the most intelligent way to ease into
the mounting sensations. Then LSD fully reached my brain
and snickered at me doing yoga and authoritatively cleared
the air and said, "Ha. I run this show now."

Reality arrived to me differently, with the tranquility
and poise of a lily pad on water. I lost the faculty I usually
liked to employ, keeping track of everything I was
experiencing. Everything reached me fresh and pure. I
stepped around the room in an exceptionally clear-minded
stupor. We flirted for a couple of hours with reality as she
removed mask after mask through the moments. I spent
hours pacing around the room, adjusting to the mindful care
I had for myself and my surroundings. Finally, Wyatt proposed we go outside.

Both of my friends encouraged me to bring a jacket.
"I'm comfortable right now. Why would I need a jacket?" I
plainly announced my confusion.

"Bro, it's forty-nine degrees outside," Wyatt responded.

"How do you have any way of knowing what the tem-
perature is outside if you're standing right here next to me?"
After a ten-minute boycott, I conceded and crept cozily into
my down jacket.

I pushed open the lobby doors of Gramercy Green, and the city arrived to me as if it had been conceived in an instant. This New York was foreign and charming. This New York was not the same city I knew energetically and synergistically. The city sang an aria instead of wailing. It invited instead of taunted. But this was New York.

There was a translucent grid against the blue sky. Every being we passed, whether a dog, human, or bird, had a dear purpose in this grid. We headed toward Madison Square Park, the closest we could come to a meadow of wildflowers in Manhattan.

Approaching an attractive young woman on the sidewalk came with the familiar feeling of wanting to greet her, but as she passed, so did I, happily. I was grateful for my head's naturally facing direction as we deftly traversed the metropolitan blocks like jets ducking and soaring. I looked up again at the translucent grid of lines in the sky.

No intrusive thoughts came that I would be better off looking behind me—I had a faint memory that I'd previously struggled with doing so. I just giggled when I remembered this. The world that seduced me as I discovered it and held me was ahead of me, not behind me.

We spent what could have been minutes or hours birdwatching and bird-communing. We ate cheeseburgers and fries from the burger shack inside the park. Wyatt placed my order for me after I said, "I want tomatoes, I want beef, I want... cheese, bread, ketchup, lettuce. Yeah. Thanks." The three of us shared a sundae. After one or two bites each, I barbarically plunged the five fingers of my left hand into the cup and left them there until I felt I had claimed the dessert.

The whole table burst into uproarious laughter. Wyatt wiped happy tears from his eyes as he said, "Well, I guess that's yours now."

We returned to Imran's and my dorm room as the sun was setting. During the denouement of the trip, it dawned on me that I had no way of using English to describe what I was experiencing. I was troubled by this but found a cathartic way through.

As I pondered the absence of a definition for this day, I arrived at a thought: *I will be asleep later tonight. Sleep is the only universal switch in consciousness that everyone goes through. If I'm going to be asleep later, then I'm alive now.* I professed my developing concepts to my friends as if behind a podium. I couldn't just burn like the sun in all my glory. I needed to bring the moon to mind to recall that I was anything, that I was alive that evening. I didn't know where this epiphany would take me, but I knew I was onto something. As I stepped down from the podium after dominating the room with my feverish thoughts, I finished with, "Dude... sleep."

Wyatt didn't understand; he just laughed and softly shook his head. Twenty minutes later, Wyatt shared with us in his chest-centered voice, "It's really interesting because Imran has a more analytical approach, whereas you have a more expressive approach." I brought my attention outside of myself and noticed what Imran was doing for the first time during the trip. He looked like he was keeping his euphoria contained while creating notes on his phone to learn from his experience and have insights for later. Meanwhile, I played with woven shirts from my closet, took a long shower, almost drowned my laptop, and philosophized about slumber. Wyatt was right.

"So your two experiences are essentially opposites," Wyatt finished. Were our experiences that distinct? Were they incompatible? Was I hogging attention throughout the day with my expressive approach?

I looked into Imran's eyes and saw a galaxy of profundity. I tried to start a conversation but could only mutter, then audibly whined. I feared that if I kept looking into his eyes, I would see he was having a more involved experience than I was, which would intensify my journey. I dropped the eye contact. I loved my best friend, but I didn't have a single conversation with him during our shared nine-hour trip on LSD.

17
Easy Street

I woke up the following morning feeling an alien, exciting lucidity. In the immediate aftermath of my psychedelic day, I started feeling no need to schedule with Dr. Layton. Each morning, I awoke with a clarity of mind. I began testing myself to see how far into a day I could stride without taking my medication in the morning. It turned out I could last a full day, then a week, until I was no longer taking my prescribed medication. Getting high on marijuana was still a regular part of my experience, but I was shocked I could handle daily life without Prozac.

September marked the advent of my junior year. It was time for "advanced training." ETW happily welcomed me back into its adoring and spiritually conscious culture. I socialized with new people, creating friendships with the students who had transferred to ETW for their advanced training. I read Mark Twain's essays in my free time. I was happy. I was doing well.

My junior year emphasized scene work more than any of the previous foundational and exploratory semesters. The work of Samuel Beckett and Anton Chekhov breathed with such mysterious beauty. The work of Annie Baker and Caryl Churchill sang with articulate power. I watched my peers become formidable "athletes of the heart," as Antonin Artaud defined the actor. I understood the script was a means to communicate truthfulness as I saw it, but I had never been so bombarded by an adoration for good writing before.

I developed more interest in what I gleaned from reading the playwrights: their timeless wishes, the truth they were composing when their sweat and ideas met paper. I was more fascinated by reading the script than performing it. I was almost insulted by the part of the creative process whereby I was to embody a character and make the words my own. The character was hogwash to me. I was rediscovering my dearest love from first grade until I discovered acting three years later: writing.

I credited LSD with clearing so many psychic cobwebs because little else was new or different enough in my life to create such a tremendous change in me. LSD effectively evaporated depressive tendencies I'd had since I was a teenager. Since high school, feeling depressed was always the wide, gray netting that caught me when I lost my footing in my various pursuits of happiness. After encountering LSD, there was no more easy access point to lowness and dejection waiting for me.

Imran had the opportunity to room with a lifelong friend from Mauritius, and he snatched the opportunity. He got to share an American home with a buddy from his native country for the first time. They lived in midtown Manhattan in a swanky place I visited a few times a month.

I found an unfurnished hovel of a bedroom in a recently renovated apartment in Bushwick. Living in Brooklyn was no almighty Manhattan—it was more neighborly, less glamorous, and breathed at a more organic pace. The shift in my environment was a splendid treat. The sky was more visible in Brooklyn, and I lived next to a park—still the closest New York came to having wild meadows.

Sure, I shared the apartment with four others, yet they were in their thirties, and nobody knew each other besides the couple who shared the basement level. The rest of us mostly holed up in our rooms, making small talk when I needed to fill a cup with water or wine, as someone else cooked dinner for themselves.

It was hard to recall that OCD is a chronic disorder as I relished hours of drawing in my room, recording myself freestyle rapping over YouTube beats, ordering my go-to combo meals with my favorite employees at the neighborhood Checkers, and picking up my first college job as an on-demand dog walker. I was happy. I was doing well.

I was accepted to the first internship of my life, a Shakespeare theater company just an hour and a half north of my hometown, in Marin County, California. There were nine fellow interns, and we were guaranteed a small role in the two shows produced over the summer, *Much Ado About Nothing* and *The Three Musketeers*.

The only caveat to this opportunity was that I had to drive there. Alone.

18
Bowing on the Road

The company performed in a spacious amphitheater at the height of dusk that descended into starlight as the play's motion accelerated. We interns also received voice and movement classes in a dedicated rehearsal space and studied Shakespearean text under the tutelage of an eighty-year-old man who was an eccentric, lifelong Shakespeare scholar.

The company's artistic director had a baby's plump cheeks, a full white beard, and a long ponytail. At one of the first meetings of the season, the director proclaimed his feelings for the town where he lived and worked, San Rafael: "I've been all around the world searching for the most beautiful place on earth, and man... this is it!" He threw open his arms and grinned like a man who was a child at heart. I agreed with him about the beauty, character, and location of the Northern California town. But I didn't care much for its distance from my home.

The commute from my mother's house to the theater company was an hour and a half. I made it in my 1998 Toyota Camry, the Christmas gift I received from my mother when I was seventeen. The highway that took me there, I-280, winds around golden hills with miles of wild sprouting grasses that turn green and become food for cattle in the spring; the freeway also offers awe-inspiring views of fog clouds rolling over the San Mateo hills.

I thoroughly enjoyed reacquainting myself with the drive I took dozens of times as a kid to spend the day in San Francisco. I appreciated the uncommon beauty of this popular highway for three days before I started noticing just how popular the roadway was. About twenty minutes into my fourth trip up to the internship on 280, I felt a surge in discomfort.

This familiar ache in my gut made me somewhat frantic in my attentiveness. It came from realizing I failed to acknowledge that I was not alone on this drive. An unfathomable variety of fellow commuters and travelers surrounded me. It took making the journey a routine for me to notice I wasn't sharing my enjoyment of this drive with any of my fellow travelers. A pesky need to include the other drivers of I-280 in my pleasure, to share the bounty of enjoyment I found on this drive, gnawed at my brain and didn't go away.

I started taking stock of the people within the cars. How dare I judge a book by its cover, or in this case, a traveler by their vehicle? I cherished my neighbors and was not about to make an exception here just because my neighbors were in rapid motion. I cherished the peeks I got into the side windows at the drivers flanking me. I could only see them from the shoulders up, but this didn't matter.

I glanced over to the person in a silver sedan to my right. I saw a woman shuffling through something on her passenger seat and then locking her gaze on the road's horizon. I noticed an empty car seat in the back. I soberly said to myself, "This person is living her life." Though we were all traveling eighty miles per hour, give or take, I continued telling myself, "It's a life in motion, but it's still a life worth considering." This realization began to make me queasy. I ruminated, *I will likely never see this person again, and I'm just going to pass her by without acknowledging her meaningfully? How could I?*

I hadn't experienced any noticeable or detracting obsessive-compulsive symptoms in a full school year, so I didn't detect that there was anything unhealthy about my thought pattern or what I did next. I was just stepping into an opportunity to be especially altruistic to people who typically communicated by flipping each other off or ignoring one another altogether. I brought the driver with the car seat to mind as she accelerated past me. I said the words, "Peace and love for you."

A rippling satisfaction overcame me once I uttered this well-intended and almost meditative phrase. I was proud that I eased my discomfort and honored a stranger's presence at the same time. This pride lasted for a few minutes.

Yet again, I was tempted into communing simply because these were strangers: *a sampling of humanity at large.* I felt embraced as if by a sea of friends-to-be. They were in their cars, separated from me, yet I felt supported because they were all around me. They helped make it impossible for me to feel completely alone.

I turned my head to a man in a Lexus SUV I was passing. From what I could see through his tinted windows, he had silvery hairs in his sideburns. I took a moment to wonder if what I was about to do again was compulsive, but I figured it couldn't be because it was so respectful. To honor this driver's presence and to thank him for being one of many to make me feel not completely alone on the drive, I said, "Peace and love for you," and nodded my head with him in mind: this time, a couple of minutes of cinched satisfaction.

There were cars everywhere, not a single one without at least one living soul inside, and they all deserved acknowledgment in some spiritual and authentic way. I felt called to provide this without hesitation or inhibition. I nodded and muttered to drivers on either side of me for the entire drive up to San Rafael. This behavior's barrel was bottomless.

Thirty minutes after crossing the Golden Gate, I was in San Rafael. I parked in front of our rehearsal space. I emerged from the car, intensely dizzy. The world outside me wasn't spinning, but my internal world was utterly disoriented. I walked into the space. My fellow interns were having clever and warm banter with each other. Their energy was perky and open. Most were stretching, rehearsing monologues with each other, or sipping coffee. As I faced the challenge of trusting and playing with my fellow interns, I found I was devoid of generosity. I had spilled it all over the freeway for an hour and a half.

I made this commute for half of my summer, and my devotion to every Joe and Jane in their car did not diminish. The nod and phrase became insufficient as I discovered my warmest regards to my neighbors could be warmer and more genuine.

The next day, the driver of a zippy yellow sports car squeezed through the spaces between cars and zoomed ahead. I knew I would never see this person again, so I wanted to send him my best wishes and do it impeccably. I took my right hand off the steering wheel, my right palm facing to my left, as in half of a prayer gesture, nodded my head, and said a more devout prayer, "Peace and love for you."

I was getting the hang of this and figured I didn't have to practice meditation or prayer in my off-time because I had picked up this new habit. What was the difference between this and a spiritual practice?

After the yellow sports car was out of sight, a few minutes later, the insatiable demands of my repetitive thoughts insisted that I take both hands off the steering wheel and steer with my knee. I offered proper prayer hands, with no part of my palms on the steering wheel, and held my hands up to my forehead, my third eye, while nervously catching glimpses of the road racing underneath me. I nodded from this position and again let my prayerful phrase leave my mouth.

I came to a consensus with my inner monologue that the bowing of my head was frivolous compared to how I could upgrade it. I looked at a nearby commuter wearing a suit in a little Honda sedan. I got my best sense of the road's trajectory ahead and made a deep bow. "So much peace and love for you," I emphatically stated, chin pointing toward my navel and my eyes on my crotch. I pulled myself from the grip of delivering well-wishes, looked in front of me, and slammed on the brakes.

I nearly collided with the rear of an SUV that had stopped ahead of me while my eyes were elsewhere. When my safety and those of others around me were in jeopardy, I had to engage in a refreshingly unfamiliar thinking style: life-and-death instinct. After thanking whatever higher power protected the integrity of my car and the lives of those around me, my following reaction was profound gratitude for simply getting to feel my survival instinct kick in. It was such a relief in contrast to the absurdly complex and esoteric ritual I had developed in the car.

Once traffic flowed like usual again, the wicked machinery in my head recommenced its operations. As long as I didn't look away from the road for too long, my verbal love letters had to be more enthusiastic. The bow had to be more genuine.

I needed my messages to the souls around me to be more varied, so I didn't always bow from then on; I alternated bending over with using both hands to form a prayer gesture held against my head or heart while I steered with one knee. Then I cried, "So much love for you! So much peace!"

After weeks of feeling like I barely looked at the road or enjoyed the tranquility of the golden hills around me during my commute, I became aware that this ritual was swelling to an untenable significance. I was fully aware that my actions were doing no real good for me and were painstakingly chipping away at the logic in my brain (not to mention putting my and others' lives on the line). I knew it, but I couldn't shake it.

I was gathered with the other interns backstage (an inlet of the woods with couches and snacks) during a dress rehearsal for *Much Ado About Nothing*. I suddenly and slowly said, "Love… in the time of cholera." I had only seen the cover of the book somewhere. I hadn't read it.

Someone heard me make one of these rare self-initiated comments of mine and asked, "Why did you say that?"

I replied, "Oh, it's a book by an author who won the Nobel Prize."

"I know what it is, but why did you say it?"

"I don't know. It just came to mind."

Reason hadn't caught up to my mouth saying it, but I knew there had to be a reason this literary phrase had threaded itself into my unconscious mind, and I felt a need to say it. Talented and dazzlingly friendly young people surrounded me. I felt I was at a disadvantage. I had an illness that manipulated my will and hindered my ability to be intimate with the people who were actually in my day-to-day surroundings. My illness stultified my spontaneity. I adored those who came to San Rafael to learn more about Shakespearean text and let their skills shine, but I had a miserable time trying to embody that love. I had no idea at the time what Gabriel García Márquez's book was even about, but I knew I was exhausted, and its title evoked how I felt when I had no other way to express myself. Love in the time of cholera.

19
Without Freaking Everybody Out

After a successful run of both shows in which I had a small part and performed them smoothly, the internship with the San Rafael theater company came to an end halfway through the summer. I reached out to Wyatt and Imran because I needed some time with the guys. Wyatt had already been planning a trip to Southern California to visit Pepperdine University in Malibu and Cal Poly in San Luis Obispo, where the other two guys from our high school friend group had gone to college.

I asked Wyatt if Imran could come. The initial plans hadn't included him because the reunion was solely for us boys from the Bay. Imran and Wyatt got along well. Wyatt, of course, had supervised Imran during his first acid trip, a long day in which Imran looked to Wyatt for guidance and security. Wyatt had found some inspiration in seeing how Imran responded to the substance. They had hung out on multiple occasions over the year I lived with Imran. I detected hints of jealousy from Wyatt, though, at the wonderment and relaxation Imran inspired in me that Wyatt never seemed to tap into when alone with me.

Wyatt was quite different from me. His voice was always full and loud, his head up, his chest out, and his confidence soaring. He was a born leader (we all just got lucky that he led mostly compassionately and not sporadically and selfishly). He and I had a thorough loyalty and history going for us, whereas what kept Imran and me close was our fascination with each other and the respect we continually nourished. Wyatt had nothing to be jealous of. We could all get along, and I wanted to prove it by bringing Imran with me on the week-long trip on the West Coast.

We got Imran so high that on a drive through the canyons of Malibu, he swore he saw ghosts and detailed just how they looked while we all listened, and some cracked up laughing.

Before any of our once-in-a-lifetime antics ensued, however, on day three of the vacation, we gave up on the crummy college food we had been eating at Pepperdine and went out to a nice restaurant in Malibu. We all sat at a table in the Malibu eatery's shaded outdoor seating area. Well, all except Imran. He stayed behind because he wanted to sleep, he told us. More likely, he had indulged in too much weed first thing in the morning and didn't want to go out in public.

Every guy I was close with in high school and I gathered at the table. We sat atop waves that lapped up against the restaurant's walls just yards beneath us. As we waited for our meal to be served, the conversational tidbits flew like pebbles from a slingshot. My friends' idiosyncratic minds conversed with such elation and overlap that, from my view, it was as if they had forgotten that they were distinct at all from each other. They were one massive heap of messy happiness, souls dancing with revelry without any regard for decorum.

If Imran had been there, I may not have said what I said next. In fact, it was the first thing I uttered since sitting down at the restaurant. There was a lull in the whizzing of conversational shrapnel over the table. My skin started tingling once this pause came because I had been waiting for a chance to speak my piece for days. Now it was here. As my friends sipped their drinks and waited to be inspired to move on to the next topic, my need to capitalize on the silence overtook me.

"You know what I realize?" I asked loudly. Their eyes landed on me, and I looked down as I took my time. This already felt like it was going awry. Still, I said what I intended to say: "I don't really talk about myself."

Wyatt looked across the table at me with his compassionate, earnest eyes and said, "Well, talk about yourself, man."

I quickly realized how much easier this was said than done. Wyatt gave his sensible response without hesitation. But the way he said it, combined with everybody's eyes on me, felt like I was suddenly stepping into a competitive challenge—a challenge I didn't know how to meet.

"Well, there's not a lot going on with me," I pitifully coughed up. "I just notice I do a lot of listening and don't really talk about myself much. Like, we guys have fun together, but I feel like you guys don't really know what's going on with me. And I just feel like it's difficult to bring up what's happening in my life without sounding super selfish."

"Well, what's going on in your life, man?" Wyatt asked then, curious and endearing. Everyone else shifted in their seats and examined their beer glasses.

"Well, not a ton," I lied, feeling like squirming away from myself and trying on someone else's skin. "There are some things that I definitely struggle with, but it's kind of hard to put them into words, actually."

I had envisioned my first declaration striking all of us like a catharsis and coming to connect with my friends over the humor and tragedy that I held back for seven years. This was not going how I envisioned. But this was new to me: speaking my mind unprompted. I felt proud that I began verbalizing how stuck and fake I had been feeling. But I couldn't develop the thought into something we could all participate in as badly as I wanted to. I felt selfish before I even got the ball rolling. I wanted to retreat again as soon as I put my hat in the ring.

I looked around at my friends, who said nothing. I wondered if they even agreed with my perception that I didn't produce much self-focused conversational content.

Wyatt asked a few more questions. He was not about to let me feel ashamed for having spoken up for myself. He persisted and waited for me to go on. I did not go on. How does one make a life understood when it has been so internal for so many years, without freaking everybody out or making them feel unimportant?

My buddies resumed flinging the conversational artillery shortly thereafter. No one could *be me for me* ever. It was up to me to find a way to voice my concerns, struggles, and ideas. I was glad I didn't suffer in silence during this lunch, and that I took a positive baby step toward transparency with this group I had spent years coming to know. I realized I didn't have to be perfectly adept at talking about myself after having virtually no practice at it for most of my life.

Of my friends, Wyatt understood the meaning behind my stammering speech the best. He knew me better than any of them. He was the one who even led me to water. But he couldn't force me to drink.

20
Inundated

It was morning. This meant the first thoughts of the day were arousing to assault me, and soon after my eyes opened, they did. Invisible yet toxic layers of dust coated every surface in my hovel of a room. I resentfully accepted the dust, but I did not allow myself to bring any of it with me outside.

Outside, the world was flawless. Crisp breezes floated by that were the opposite of dusty. But inside my puny residence, the same Bushwick apartment where I used to read and freestyle rap to my heart's content, everything from my bed to my closet was inundated with microscopic dust that I accepted as my personal weight to bear.

Bringing any of the particles with me into the outer world was a petrifying idea. The dust had such dark power that it would destroy the sidewalk, leaving only rubble if it fell from my clothing outside. Hence, I developed a pressing concern for purifying the clothing in my closet from the dust that threatened to toxify my beautiful neighborhood. I got out of bed with urgency. One of the few trusty privileges I had that brightened my perspective was that I was beleaguered with anxiety rather than sunk in depression (a preference I maintained throughout college). Still, the state of my mind was not well.

The alternation of compulsions and healthy behavior that punctuated passing time for me was a past phenomenon. Now, my obsessive thoughts had fattened themselves up like prize-winning pigs. My compulsive behaviors were now on par with, if not more important than, my instinct. OCD was wringing its hands around my organs and usurping the power of my gut; it was rebranding my core instinct as its vehicle for its wishes. But all this was occurring inside me. Who was to say I could do anything to stop it?

I strode across the room, reluctantly stirring up some of the dust with my footsteps. I grabbed a pair of underwear from my drawer. I did a little spin on the balls of my feet to face the same direction I always faced when I did the ceremonial clothing of myself. I imitated my mother's snappy whooshing motion whenever she pulled a top sheet out of a dryer. She brought it up as high as her arms would go, then quickly down, letting the sheet flow against air resistance. Now, I did just that and yet had no connection to a purposeful behavior. I raised my underwear above my head and swooshed it down with a snap. I did that again. I did that five more times. Then, I did it about fifteen more times.

I shook out a pair of jeans forty times. Maybe it was more. I was not keeping count; I was only waiting to reach utter defeat or to feel that bitter inner bell ding that marked completion for that piece of clothing. Carrying a backpack with me into the city was in my plans, yet some inner voice told me the backpack wasn't as toxified with dust as my clothing was. The clothing was what required absurdly rigorous attention. If I had been shaking out my clothing to mend a broken heart, the exerted muscles and the innumerable repetitions of the act would likely bring burning tears to my eyes. But this was not an emotional experience. It just had to be done right. It was all about designing the most efficient path possible through the devastating orders.

A shirt, a pair of socks, and a jacket: these articles of fabric colonized my mornings.

When I saw visible dust fall from the clothing, I chuckled. It was not the sight of actual dust leaving the clothing I was after. It was the befuddling dust I could not see. This type was also the only kind that could obliterate the Brooklyn sidewalk.

And that was the prodding motivator behind all of this. I couldn't be the one to leave behind an altogether irresponsible and disastrous line of rubble as I walked. I couldn't do that to my city or my neighbors. They had to be able to walk on that sidewalk. With that premise settled into my head like an ancient shipwreck forgotten at the bottom of the ocean, I kept shaking everything out until hours into my morning routine, I was dressed.

All the knowledge I had earned through both observation and experience over the past few years was under a genocidal attack as OCD battered it into all but oblivion. I still had a personality, but barely. I had creative instincts, but they were awfully confused.

My long observance of having to put on "safe" clothing earned me several tardy arrivals to class, sometimes by an hour or more. I told no one about what I was caught up in on my way there, and took the below-average marks in stride. There was one way I could leave the house. I let abysmal attendance grades become part of my destiny.

I didn't speak to Dr. Layton this semester; however, I did resume phone calls to my parents. The bizarre law that governed that nobody on the West Coast could relate to my experiences because of all the farmland and distance between us had retreated into remission. I assumed hyper-responsibility as I always had, but spiritually, I was on my knees and desperate for any support from someone who knew me. I was avoiding hanging out with Wyatt and Imran. I had fallen completely out of touch with Emily, Moriah, and Electric.

During this first semester of senior year, I resumed my side gig as an on-demand dog walker. I found the jobs through an app on which I marked on a map where and when the dog pooped and peed for the owner to celebrate from their end of the app.

This evening, I selected an hour-long dog walk with a well-off husky mix. We moseyed through the dog's upscale Brooklyn apartment complex along the water. During the stroll, I was free to converse with whomever I wanted to, and I spent the entire hour talking to my dad.

I listened to his exciting updates from life in Central America. He had moved to Costa Rica once I left for college. As he told me about his gigs editing and writing in Spanish and English for a local newspaper and a tourist guide, I had to be honest with him and interject. I was suffering from the ripples of a compulsion that I had left incomplete. What I told him was I was feeling "distracted." I was actually feeling the empirical pull to return to my room to address the unfinished portion of a compulsive process. I detailed an obsessive-compulsive symptom of mine to my father for the first time. It just so happened that the reason I could not give my father my full attention was because of a symptom that was the most impossible to navigate of them all.

Every morning, the curtain at the head of my bed was closed in front of the window that looked out onto the street from my floor-level street-facing apartment. I became the host of a parasitic fear that, as I opened the curtain, the world's power was entering my room, not just sunlight. This energy was critical in deciding whether I would have a happy social life in my home stretch of college. Despite all the social reservations I embodied in my previous days, I wanted a healthy social life more than anything at this point. I hungered for the surprises, the conversation, advice, lessons, and humor from friends. How I responded to the dizzyingly powerful orb of energy that came in through the window was the highest-level determinant of my ability to leave college with real friends.

I inhaled all the opalescent, sizzling energy into my left shoulder, the only container I believed could hold this elemental power. I then turned around and shot the world's power onto my wall thrice by jutting the same shoulder forward like a semiautomatic rifle. The energy landed as three discs on the wall; I then had to reabsorb the energy back into my body, not with my shoulder this time, but with the muscles around my eyes and eyebrows. I had to reclaim it because these discs of potential energy were as threatening to be without as they were to be with.

So, as I walked the affluent dog through his neighborhood, I told my father that I left one of the discs of energy on the wall in my hurry to make it to the dog walk before the job was given to someone else. I explained that this oversight gnawed at me as I tried to express my genuine excitement for my father's enjoyment of his paradise country.

My dad listened attentively and patiently. He found my bizarre symptoms fascinating and let me know he felt for me. He had sympathy toward me, not just puzzlement. He let me know he was thoroughly supportive of my recovery journey. He didn't offer direct counsel (if he had, it probably would have done more harm than good), but he was a pair of ears and a source of levity—both of which I needed desperately.

I didn't learn that my deranged process of stewarding the world's energy was ineffective; it was genuinely my only hope. If I didn't complete the ritual error-free, I directly summoned a feeling of unpreparedness so radical that I would sooner refuse to leave my house than represent myself to potential friends with such a disgraceful incompletion on my personal record.

21
Festering

I was constantly being handed pamphlets on the sidewalks of Manhattan and Brooklyn. Sometimes, I audaciously turned them down and kept walking, but most of the time, I wanted the people distributing them to feel like they were there for a good reason. So, I took the handout politely with a feigned smile. I carried these pamphlets in my backpack from NYU back to Brooklyn. When I got to my apartment, I slid them under my mattress frame.

Upon getting home, I ordered food from an online delivery service: shrimp pad Thai. After finishing my meal, I felt it would be cruel and aggressive to throw away the shrimp tails. I placed them under my bed as well. Unwittingly, I was re-experiencing a burgeoning commitment to self-destructive behavior. But I feared partaking in what I saw as a violent process: deciding what was and was not trash. Determining what was to be destroyed or sustained was a question I wanted no part in. I stopped throwing things away. Before I knew it, I was accompanied by enormous black trash bags that sustained my sense of safety but looked like rotund corrections officers. I stuffed the bags to their limits with items I refused to part with. I was not going to be the executioner of anything. *The aggression of throwing things away would obviously spread to being destructive in other areas of life,* I heard myself think.

I absorbed the subsequent fear like a pupil at his desk: I feared transferring my trash from one receptacle to another, from my wastebasket to a garbage bag. When it was time to do this, I had to reinspect the contents of the wastebasket item by item, despite the gall I had summoned to toss them in there in the first place. This was no matter; I had to revisit every candy wrapper, old piece of homework, pamphlet, and shrimp tail and memorize its structural and textural details. What choice did I have if I was next throwing these items into a raging incinerator?

During the task of transferring the trash out of my wastebasket, I encountered an avocado shell. The shell had been in my room for weeks and had become festering with blue mold.

I severed the umbilical cord between myself and any awareness I had of my gut instinct to be freaked out. Instead, I studied the shell's unique features for a good twenty seconds, doing my best to let my fingers only touch where there was no mold on the outside. During this series of long seconds, I told myself that this was a natural piece of flora; *everything natural is a thing of beauty,* I reminded myself requisitely. Once I had memorized its "story," as it were, I let it fall into the black garbage bag and held back gagging as I rushed to wash my hands.

Eight industrial-sized garbage bags filled the floor of my room and claimed the chaise lounge. The bags comforted me, proof that I was a pacifist with objects. No one knew I was saving every bit of rubbish that crossed my path. *So I couldn't be a hoarder, right?*

But the garbage emitted a stench.

One of my male roommates asked about the smell via our apartment group text. He messaged, "Nathan, what's that terrible smell coming from your room?"

I took advantage of the fact that my read receipts were off and took some time to get back to the text. I finally crafted what I saw as an artful and open-minded response: "Why do you ask?"

Him, back: "Because when I smell something that smells like a dead cat coming from my roommate's room, I want to fucking know what it is."

I typed back, "I'm experiencing some personal issues right now and working on throwing away some trash." I was honest but not so precise as to risk being thought crazy or having a hoarding problem.

Night had fallen hours ago, and it was time to sleep. I stepped around the Glads and Heftys, which were half my height. Finally, I lunged over the loose trash—a fraction of my collection—that I kept packed under the bed frame. I closed my eyes. As I was falling asleep, I heard the sound of mice or rats scurrying across the floor and tearing through the plastic garbage bags with their teeth. I was tired. I didn't have the energy required to invoke the panic I felt simmering in my chest. The idea that all that was natural was beautiful apparently made no exception for vermin.

So, I let the mice eat what they could find. After ten minutes of the gnawing keeping me awake, I got up to turn on my lights. I confirmed they were mice, not rats, and returned to bed, thankful that my mattress stood a couple of feet from the floor.

As I drifted to sleep, I imagined the reaction of the young British woman who lived in the basement with her husband if she were to happen into my room and nearly step on one of the mice. She would scream bloody murder and race out of sight, shrieking once down the hall, "We need an exterminator, like, yesterday!" Too many compulsions lay in wait between the comfort I felt in my bed and calling pest control at this hour.

I woke up the following day to a rodent-free room and garbage bags with mouse-sized holes pierced in their sides. My initial response was one of gladness that the New York mice had absconded with top-tier finds. I knew they'd be back. Maybe I'd shriek in disgust tomorrow.

22
Beyond Certain

During our phone calls, my mother pleaded with me to resume my sessions with Dr. Layton, the woman who guided me toward recovery more deftly than anyone else in my life. I told her it wouldn't do any good, that my symptoms had infested my daily lifestyle so thoroughly that therapy wouldn't be any help. Plus, when Dr. Layton and I were working together, I mostly learned a lot about the efficacy of treatment without letting myself see that treatment could be effective.

At the same time, I was compulsively saying phrases in the shower to send away fears that I would lose touch with my body under the warm water. I turned the phrase "no shit" into a chant I made hundreds of times a day to protect myself in any number of situations. It took me three hours to get dressed every morning.

I'd had enough. I made the call.

I was surprised to see a text from Dr. Layton the following morning that read like she was happy to hear from me. I accepted one of the open appointment slots she offered me, and suddenly, I was back in the game.

I gave myself two hours to get ready and make it to her office on the Upper East Side. In the shower, I repeated aloud, "I'm cleaning my body now, in a way... But that's not the *point*." I had to repeat the word *point* like a police dog biting into a suspect's leg harder and harder every time. My showers filled thirty minutes of the morning.

The first time the phrase "no shit" left my mouth in years was when I stepped around a leaf unnaturally to avoid it. I said the phrase as a tool to convince myself that my leaf avoidance was not, in fact, symptomatic. The two words, "no shit," multiplied like ambitious bacteria and left my mouth throughout the day. My use of the phrase eventually became more like word soup: I said "no sh-yeah, no sh-yeah" for short once, and it stuck. This lingo was my protector from the most minuscule to the most maximal anxiety-inducing triggers in a day.

I stopped in my doorway before leaving my bedroom. I raised and lowered my arm like Fred Astaire practicing scales on set with flair and chanted "no sh-yeah, no sh-yeah" melodically about four times.

I put the key in the lock of the apartment door and turned it, but didn't pull it out. I stared at the key in the keyhole and continued to chant my jargon while my heels were itching to move on. I regurgitated the mantra until it was safe to put the key in my pocket.

I approached my senseless ceremonies with the heart of a performer. I didn't let any line be a throwaway. I shaped every compulsive behavior so that it not only satisfied me, but if it were to be seen by another, it would at least be eye-catching, if not transfixing. I didn't feel one of the most common responses to living with OCD: *shame*. My compulsive habits didn't only mean protection but also indicated my individuality—they were what made me me.

I arrived at Dr. Layton's office building thirty minutes late for our appointment.

I stopped being flung by harassing compulsions when I sat down in the waiting room sofa chair.

The sensation of coming to rest after my long journey restored my compulsivity before it restored me with wakefulness. As I sat in the chair, I thought exclusively of all the potential energy I was storing in the seat, a kind of energy that would be perilous to leave behind. Layton walked out wearing a long, black sweater dress. Her warm face was still discerning. Her made-up lips parted in a smile. She called me into her office. I touched the bottom of the seat a few times, so I could retain my ability to enjoy rest. Once we sat down, I could see on her face that she could tell I was markedly worse off. When the session got rolling, and I was back in a space where self-acceptance and self-examination were central, that chair in the waiting room bellowed to me. Nearly bowing, like the lady in Phoenix who had hosted my dad and me when I was a kid, I scuttled out of the room as I said, "I'll be right back." We were only a few minutes into the session. I left her office and sat in the same chair that I had been in minutes earlier. I touched the seat differently this time. Then I stayed there.

I spent a minute touching the seat, not ready to recommence the difficult therapeutic journey of acknowledging the dark dysfunctions that were masticating me and getting ready to swallow. Dr. Layton poked her head through the doorway and found me sitting there, trying to catch my breath and scavenging for some composure. I plainly denied that leaving her office a few minutes into our session was a compulsion. I said it was merely "a choice."

"Long time no see!" she said in a tone without malice or sarcasm as we finally sat down and mutually understood the session had started.

"Yeah," I replied.

My eyes darted around as if they were twitching. I was reviewing all the rituals I skipped on the way to her office and envisioned myself going back and doing them correctly. It was a desperate mental plunge, my sincerest attempt to adequately meet her in the room.

"I'm only going to be able to give you a twenty-minute session today. You were thirty minutes late, as you know." She paused. "Is your lateness to today's session due to compulsions you're spending time doing on your way here?"

"Yeah," I said, with some guilt and bitterness that she saw right through my behavior. I felt like I was on trial in a criminal case, and she was the judge, but she was just looking out for me.

I suffered in my seat as I sat across from her. While I spoke to her, her visage was tense and patient. She slightly winced and empathetically frowned at whatever visible tension or distress she saw in me. I plumbed down with integrity and told her what was going on with the dust, mustering enough details for her to get the concept.

She said, "So this sounds like a contamination fear."

This identification came completely out of the blue. I was not expecting her to categorize it as such.

"Right, you have this fear that you will contaminate the ground by dropping dust on it," she went on.

"Well, more like a fear I'll destroy it. Like I'll just leave a path of rubble behind me if I don't shake out my clothing, and that's scary to me."

"Yeah. It is. Well, a contamination obsession can be any unwanted thought that leads you to fear something will bring harm to someone or something else when they come in contact with each other. For you, the sidewalk is coming under harm."

"Okay. Right," I said. I didn't care at that point what it was called. I just knew it was all-consuming, and I couldn't see myself stopping it anytime soon.

She somehow saw right through my curt words and felt my level of discomfort. She closed the distance between us by handing me a sheet of homework, as she had at the close of all of our sessions. But as she handed me the homework, she looked down, which she never did. She seemed sad that she had not been working with me during the proliferation of my symptoms. I heard in her tone—that had never been so soft—that she felt less faith that she could lead me to a healthy lifestyle. She had less faith that she could be the one to rein in the beast that had hold of me.

"I have another client at 3:00, Nathan. I'm sorry I can't accommodate you for a longer session," she declared gently.

"That's okay. Thank you," I replied.

A few sessions later, Dr. Layton began without pretense: "Nathan, I'm not sure that our work together solely will be sufficient for you to get better." She had to get re-familiarized with my not responding when she expected me to; she continued, "I also don't think it's smart for you to be living in New York alone. I recommend you look into an inpatient treatment program for OCD."

I felt so far from her. She wanted to pass me up the chain to a deeper degree of treatment because she didn't think we had the time or that she had the power to treat my OCD.

She was in contact with my mother. My mother also started lovingly prodding me to apply to inpatient programs for OCD, which is how I found out my therapist and my mother were in cahoots for my betterment. My mother brought to my attention a few places Dr. Layton had directly recommended to her. As we discussed the plausibility of my taking time off from school when there was only one class left for me to complete, she said, "Dr. Layton told me she doesn't feel it's *safe* for you to be living alone in New York."

So, the truth was unveiled in a discussion between the two paramount women in my life. It's not that Dr. Layton thought it wasn't *smart*; apparently, she thought it was *unsafe* to be living the lifestyle I was living.

I experienced the surprise of unexpected social influence for the first time this year in conversing with these two brilliant women. The purpose of my every action this year had been to prepare myself for social surprises. Now, a casual comment over the phone that I was unprepared for and the conversation that contextualized it were exactly what helped me move into action. I accepted the help and got into a program from an interview that gave the accurate impression that I was suffering pointlessly and relentlessly. I couldn't maintain the conversation without asking the interviewer to wait for me as I removed the phone from my face and performed compulsive behavior to maintain a sense of my place in the world inside my head.

23
The Arrival

My mother's ticket was round-trip. Mine was one-way.

It was spring, my favorite season. New flowers bloomed; there was resplendent and unoppressive sunshine and nascent life. My mother and I were in the car; she drove, and I welcomed myself to Belmont, Massachusetts. The town had more than a fair share of natural beauty: tree branches formed canopies over the winding roads, and all the modest houses had sprawling front yards.

I wasn't shaking in my boots. I felt as though struck by a jolt of discipline. I always cared about being one who followed the rules and being in the good graces of an authority figure, even when I was skeptical of their style or chosen lessons. Here, I could sense that whatever practices were planned for me would be time-tested and world-class; this comprised the hearsay I received from Dr. Layton about this place, McLean Hospital. She called their OCD Institute "the best in the country for treating OCD."

Far from the cumbersome challenges of college, I was ready to follow new guidelines, even if they were to extract my entire and vast sense of security. I also felt like I was on vacation. It was a vacation that, if I worked hard enough, might save my life.

The campus looked like the milieu of a historic Ivy League college—I was bizarrely jazzed when I saw its colonial architecture and manicured lawns. I wondered which buildings David Foster Wallace, Sylvia Plath, and Ray Charles had stayed in. I had a taste for the finer things, and this looked like the finest psychiatric hospital I couldn't have imagined.

My mother parked in the lot of the administrative building, where we were instructed to check in via a string of emails. My mother and I looked at each other before stepping out of the vehicle. "Here we are, honey." She smiled endearingly.

"Let's do this," I said abruptly. I got out of the car.

I was a spaceman floating thousands of miles from home. There was a lot on my mind. Whereas I'm sure the astronaut is good at filtering out what is unnecessary, I let the nebula of thoughts breeze through me. It was rather pleasant, having unfamiliar thoughts that were exciting because they were *new*.

As I walked beside and past the dignified columns at the entrance of the building, I thought of the film *Awakenings* with Robin Williams and Robert De Niro. The film takes place in a chronic hospital. Robin Williams plays a pioneer who works to cure a seemingly incurable illness that leaves its patients catatonic. The stone pillars made me realize I had never been so close to the setting of that film as I was now.

We walked up to the desk, where a thick matte glass wall was between us and a woman. My mother nearly started to speak, but nudged me to take over. "I'm here to be an inpatient at the OCD Institute," I told the lady through the holes in the wall.

The woman pointed us to another department, which she said was at the end of a tunnel. Indeed, we had to cross through a low-ceiling, subterranean corridor until we reached the second administrative building to check in to the correct department. Reaching the second building, which had a similar vibe to the first space, finally made me feel that I was not at a prestigious university and not at a ski lodge. I was in a hospital.

I finished the paperwork with the second administrator, who directed us to a third building, which my mother and I had to access by driving across campus. Once there, a psychiatrist gave me an initial evaluation of my levels of suicidality and depression in her wood-paneled and literature-lined office.

While she was asking me questions like, "In the past two weeks, how often have you felt hopeless?" I felt other introspective questions coming my way as I acclimated myself to my surroundings. I knew in my heart of hearts that the rituals prevented me from living a full life. But I couldn't imagine a happy life without them. All I could see was the devastation of being unprepared, clueless, and scared all the time. I heard the psychiatrist ask, "How difficult is it for you to connect with people or perform at school or work?"

I answered, "extremely difficult." I had my fill of distorting the truth. Now was the time to be as transparent as possible. As I was leaving the somewhat stuffy office, I asked myself, *Am I willing to give up my comfort for the sake of my health?* I didn't have an answer yet.

We received instructions from the psychiatrist's receptionist to head to a place called "Orchard House." My mother and I exchanged skeptical glances from the corners of our eyes at the mention of the name. Her expression showed pleasant curiosity; I feared this was a terrible euphemism for the pasture I was being sent out to.

My mother and I were confused about being guided by the navigation app to turn right immediately before the hospital's exit into what looked like an actual orchard. *Apple trees?* I thought. I had no idea what was going on.

My mom asked, "Is this right?"

I stopped myself from saying *I don't know.*

"I'm not sure," I replied. With those three words, I preserved my perception of my ability to be sure in most cases.

There were about seven columns by twenty rows of trees that did not look like they bore much fruit, but were not dead either. When we reached the end of the tree plots, there towered a three-story, pure white, colonial-style house that overlooked the orchard. A proscenium of thick woods framed the house's backside. It appeared as if it were a crossover between a schoolhouse and a church from the 1920s, its highest level dwarfing most homes I had seen. It stuck out so strangely: it had no columns or brick, as all the other buildings on the McLean campus had. It was a house!

The navigation app was inching closer to the end of our route, and it appeared to be dropping us off at the beautiful structure at which we were both gazing. We both said "Wow" flatly, caught between conservatism and eagerness. We confusedly got out of the car to rap on the door.

A cheerful and warm face met us. She introduced herself as a social worker and welcomed us to "Come on in!"

I guess this is it, I thought.

The designers of Orchard House had repurposed rooms that clearly originally comprised a home and converted them into spaces where inpatients could live, eat, meet, and work.

The interior reminded me of my preschool, Alphabet Soup, which was also a converted home. It was like my first day of pre-K all over again. There was a large sink in the kitchen that the front door immediately opened into. It reminded me of the sink basin where I learned how to wash my hands as a toddler.

Beyond the kitchen was a dining room with a long, traditional wooden table that brought to mind an Alcoholics Anonymous meeting space more than my preschool. A few people sat at the table, enjoying some time off from scheduled activities.

The carpet was unmistakably institutional. It was solid red in some rooms and navy blue in others. The social worker pointed out the living room, which had a couch, a flat-screen TV, and a collection of video games and DVDs. A couple of people sitting on the sofa greeted me as if I were a puppy they had gotten for Christmas. I did my best to match their warmth, but mostly gave a timid wave and followed along with our social worker guide and my mother. The lady showing us around led us up the blue-carpeted staircase to the second floor.

"So on this floor… is where your room will be! This is it right here, actually. You can keep all your stuff in here, and you'll be rooming with Henry!" she told me.

I stepped into an empty room that was spacious, plentiful with natural light, and just like any other bedroom, apart from there being a second bed against the other wall that belonged to my roommate, whom I hadn't yet met, Henry.

I looked over at my mom, eager to share a knowing glance of how sweet this room was. Her mouth was slightly agape, and she was completely still. She even looked pale as she took in what was on the walls.

There were some handwritten signs taped up on the walls. They read, "Henry is a rapist," "Henry will become a serial killer," and "Henry will kill his parents." The pictures were drawn with a child's artistic skill, showing a family holding hands next to a bloody knife.

Luckily, I had some context that my mother lacked. This house was filled exclusively with fellow sufferers of OCD, so I soon grasped that this was some kind of technique to portray his fears. These were not plans. These thoughts plagued Henry and made him ever doubtful of his future as a serial killer-to-be.

I put a hand on my mother's back. She didn't understand. I could feel how tight her energy was.

I stepped up to my bed and dropped my bags on the floor. I knew full well my backpack was secretly stuffed with trash I had accumulated from the airport and the days pre-

168

ceding my check-in. I knew I would have to deal with that somehow. Luckily, that task wasn't happening now.

My mother and I walked downstairs. Henry was now sitting at the end of the dining table. He seemed to be on the lookout for a new guy who looked like he didn't know where he was and who would be his new roommate. Henry gave me a hearty handshake that had his whole arm flapping. He was a stocky guy with small, gentle eyes and a killer smile.

After meeting him, my mom and I continued wandering, clearly needing to verbalize something we were both struck by. "Well, he was the nicest young guy!" she exclaimed.

"Yeah, super nice and even, like... gentle," I added.

"Right?"

Our attending social worker had to fulfill other duties, including preparing more paperwork for me with her colleague. My mom and I trawled around the house. We discovered more construction paper signs similar to the ones posted in Henry's and my room throughout the house. Some of them showed skillful drawings. One said, "Jesus will forgive me if I don't always think about him." Some other therapists appeared and calmed my mother's tension when they provided the necessary context for what she was seeing.

My mother had brought me to the house where I would stay for two to six weeks. She had seen it for herself, seen me see it for myself, and now the time had come for her to leave. After hugging me long and well, she made her way back to the car. I knew my mom and could hear her silently wishing, *I hope this is the place that gets my boy back.* She gave a hearty wave to me before ducking into the car and taking off for her flight back to California.

24
The Lethargic Pace of Belmont, Massachusetts

When I was a teenager who couldn't yet drive, I often waited to meet somebody at places I didn't frequent very often, or I waited for someone with a car to pick me up from such a place. In these instances, I had the great fortune of being able to just watch the birds swirl and people hurry in front of me. Time stood still for me because I had nowhere to be. And the scene created before me became my whole world for those minutes. In these resplendent moments, I often thought, *I should do this more often: stand in a place where I'm a complete stranger and observe life unfold.* That pleasurable idleness is exactly how it felt staying in Belmont, Massachusetts. The world I saw unfolding before me was the entire world for me because I had nowhere else to be.

As I unpacked my luggage in my room, at the top of my mind was the question of which compulsive rituals would transfer over to this Northeastern, laidback milieu and which were strictly dependent on New York's design. The compulsions I had developed around boarding the subway would have to go. The rigid hesitancy I trained in myself when leaving my apartment and stopping in the middle of my block to look behind me multiple times was no longer relevant. But before I could decide which habits to keep performing here, Henry entered the room and sat on his bed across from me.

"So what's up, man?" He flashed his devilish grin. He made light talk of us both having mental issues. He said he didn't know what my symptoms were, and I could tell him only if I wanted. I said they were complicated and kind of spread through everything for me.

"I tell you what, buddy, whatever you got going on, just be glad you ain't got what I do… I mean, shit. Stuff is no joke. I never thought I had OCD. It was never on my radar. But, after years of this stuff, thinking I'm gonna kill people, I finally got a good diagnosis. OCD. Never thought it in a million years, bro. Shit's for real." He laughed heartily—a laugh that came only from knowing real pain. His chest rose and fell as he continued laughing. He worked in construction. He was so approachable. His relationship to the diagnosis of OCD was much different from mine. I suspected OCD early on in my experience, although it may have been detected earlier with some extra skepticism or examination from my parents. But this was never meant to be. I made OCD my entire identity, and mine was a secret identity.

He told me about all the crazy antics he got into with his buddies on the job, in bars, and about the debauchery they stirred up when they were on vacation on paradise islands. If I had lived through some of the times he was relaying to me, they would have been the times of my life. One of these events was just another experience for him.

He was a complete person, and he suffered in silence on the inside. He had a life, but he spent all of his time worrying that he would become a killer one day soon. Beneath the ease with which he cracked jokes and carried himself like a bucking bronco through life, that was what was going on inside him for years. Laughing with, admiring, and feeling like a fellow guy with Henry was the last guess I would have made about how my first day getting to know my roommate at a psychiatric inpatient treatment program would go.

When I told him I was at NYU and studied acting, he gladly pulled out stories of times when he produced low-budget films in LA. So, we shared an interest in filmmaking, not just our debilitating mental illness. It was the longest and most enjoyable conversation I'd had with anybody besides my parents in at least a year.

When Henry chose to go downstairs to pop one of the video games into the console in the living room, I had the large, sunny room to myself. I wanted to raise the blinds in front of the window. I wanted to see the full view, undisturbed by the angled white bars of the blinds. I dared not. Even though it wasn't a curtain, it was still a window. Changing the mechanism that blocked my view of the outside meant inviting that horrible, forceful energy into my shoulder. What I would do with it here... I refused to think about it. So, I appreciated the trees and the thick greenery across the street through the slashes of white aluminum blocking my line of sight. The perfection of leaving the stacked blinds unperturbed satisfied me so deliciously. Then, of course, I felt sad. I stepped away from the window.

I sat down on my bed, withdrew a notebook from my backpack that I had brought with me from Bushwick, and peeled it open. The creative energy within was awe-inspiring to me. I had held so much back the past year, and most of my habits were still locked in place, but now I was somewhere new that inspired me to breathe more deeply. I started writing a poem. I had to go downstairs soon to be apprised of the schedule for the week, but I put pen to paper regardless, in a celebration of instinct. I opened the poem spontaneously as an ode to young children. I wrote about people I had met and shook hands with who left the room, and whom I never saw again. I wrote, "I do not wish to offend, I do not wish to bore, but wishing with fear has done nothing but stunted galore." I addressed the young children toward the poem's end: "Be like the air, heed not my words as law / Sense me not as a father." I likely wrote that because of what I was going through then. I didn't want anyone freewheeling through their youth to be curbed by an authority figure. And I didn't want my ultimate authority figure, OCD, to have the last laugh.

If I were going to find my liberation and purity of mind in this place, however on God's green earth that was going to happen, I didn't want to succeed owing any credit to a superior. I wanted to get there thanks to my own work.

Once the clock struck 11:00 a.m., all the inpatients assembled at the house's long dining table to review the schedule for the week—standard procedure for all but me. This was my first time meeting most of these people and learning about the processes of the day here. I warmly looked across the table at the faces of diverse folks, people younger and older than me, and felt new butterflies rise in my stomach. I had to get on a subway to reach friends in New York. The distance and time separating me from potential friends suggested that I would be more firmly prepared by engaging in compulsive rituals. New people were just so magnificently *here*. They were feet away from me. It humbled me to realize this was how it was for many of these people for a while.

Standing at the head of the table was Mindy Brooks. She led the meeting. She handed out weekly agendas for everyone to reference as she discussed the activities on the calendar. I saw a large chunk of time devoted to ERP—good old exposure and response prevention therapy. Mindy clarified that the time block for ERP was four hours every day for each of us. In these sessions, we would be paired one-on-one with a therapist or graduate student who would facilitate and guide us through the work.

I automatically remembered my exposure and response prevention work in New York: paltry, half-assed steps in confronting my fears. I only did therapeutic tasks when I was asked to, and my work never yielded effects that were quite lasting. I would have a guide here. That would be... different, right?

Mindy covered other activities on the schedule. We had plenty of free time, and the rest of the time that wasn't free consisted of group classes such as sleep hygiene, mindfulness, and art therapy. There were specialized classes for people's various manifestations of OCD: intrusive thoughts, hoarding, scrupulosity, etc. These were all just titles on a piece of paper to me so far, and more came my way: family issues and relapse prevention. We would work with a social worker who would pull up family members of our choice on a video call. We would meet with a psychiatrist every week for those (like me) who were taking medication or would benefit from it if they were not. And finally, we had weekly fifty-minute sessions with our therapist.

The meeting ended, and people generally broke apart to enter a period of free time. Except Mindy pulled me aside. I thought she would just introduce herself formally to the new guy in the house, which she did, but she introduced herself as my new therapist. I was pleased because she seemed level-headed and capable. "So, Nathan, we can have our very first session right now, if you're ready?" she asked.

I had no reason not to be. "Yeah," I said. "I can do that. Where shall we have it?"

"I was thinking we could sit outside under the tree out here." She gestured to the back of the house, and outside we went.

It was a cloudless, temperate day. We sat in the house's backyard next to its garden in white Adirondack chairs beneath a tree with huge, drooping branches.

She had clear, blue eyes that communicated faith in me even while she got to know me. She asked me to start where

I was distressed: to begin with what was holding me back. The look in her eyes of soaking in information while having great confidence in me (and in her skills) helped me open up and express more of my symptoms than I ever had. I wasn't putting pressure on myself to paint an unnecessarily intricate portrait of my condition; she hadn't asked for that. She was incisive, inquisitive, and as warm as she could be as a world-class clinician.

A difference I noticed between Dr. Layton and Mindy, who encouraged me to call her by her first name, was that Mindy gained value from everything I told her. I never once felt that she was searching for the meaning behind everything I wasn't telling her, that practice of sniffing for the dysfunction behind my words. I felt that from Dr. Layton. Mindy seemed to only glean value from everything I did tell her. Her approach helped me continue opening up. Maybe she was asking the right questions; maybe it was the overall sense I had that I had traveled far to seek treatment at a world-class hospital, so I better speak up for myself because no one else would. I was ready to reveal just how much I had been suffering over the past few years.

"We can start wherever you'd like, maybe with what's been causing you pain recently?"

"Sure. So…" I began. I let myself relax in the sun-kissed chair. "I've been suffering a lot lately. I just do so many compulsions in a day, it's crazy."

Her eyes were so big and seemingly objective that I narrowed my focus and tried to be as honest as possible.

"And I don't think I've really given myself any chances to recognize the state of my life. Like, mostly, I spend my days shaking out my clothing for hours, but I also go through a lot of compulsive behavior in the shower… I don't know. I thought a lot of these symptoms would be exclusive to Brooklyn because I kind of created them specifically with and for the design of the city. But, for example, my compulsions around how I open windows are the same—" I started feeling like I was taking up too much time. "Should I start by telling you what my symptoms are more specifically?" I asked.

"You can tell me whatever you'd like; I want to gain a good sense of your history, but I want to tap into your present situation as well. I recommend you just keep going."

"Okay. So, yeah, I have the same deathly fear of opening windows as I did in Bushwick. That didn't go away just because I'm here. And I have this really drawn-out ritual with my curtain back in Brooklyn." She nodded. "And I noticed there are no curtains here, just blinds. So that'll be an interesting transition."

"Uh-huh." She smiled a bit and just listened.

"I feel lucky because I actually have a very good sense of what my actual symptoms are. Like, I can list them and name them all, basically. Like, I'm ridiculously aware of them, but I just can't stop any of them. And that's why I'm here."

"And let's go over what some of those symptoms are. What are some of the distressing thoughts you experience that come into your head unwanted?"

"Well, hm. I have an obsession that I will drop some kind of dust from my clothing that will break up the sidewalk, and as a result, I stand in my room for hours shaking out my clothing so it's dust-free in my mind. And I know it's not even real dust; it's, like, imagined dust. But it feels terrifyingly real to me."

"Okay. Great. Are there any other noticeable, unwanted thoughts that you experience regularly? Unpleasant or annoying thoughts?"

"Honestly, it's usually not an obsession that will be noticeable, but more of the compulsive side of things. Yeah."

"Okay. So you mentioned some great difficulty with opening windows and curtains." She spoke authentically, like a fine actor who made inhabiting a character look effortless because she had put in countless hours behind the scenes. I got a flash of an image of her writing a dissertation about me; she seemed so invested and caring. "When you are disturbed by opening your window at home, what is usually going on in your head? What are your thoughts telling you?"

"They're telling me that I will not be able to make friends in college if I don't do my ritual correctly."

"Okay. So it sounds like, from what I know, you are pretty familiar with the ERP work we'll be doing here, which is a branch of CBT. What was your impression of doing ERP with your previous therapist in New York?"

I told her that my therapist spent most of her time teaching me about how OCD worked and that it was difficult to invest in the treatment plan when I was on my own.

As we proceeded, she told me, "You're doing very good, by the way; I just want to let you know. I know it's hard to reveal some of your most private or even secret rituals to someone you're just meeting, but I have met with hundreds of patients with every kind of symptom imaginable. There's nothing I haven't heard. I've been working in the field of

OCD for about four years, and I am dedicated to being a resource you can reach out to, that you can confide in before and after you do your ERP sessions, four hours a day, every day."

So she had worked with people with OCD for a shorter time than Dr. Layton, but she seemed fresher, quite disciplined, and maybe more malleable in her mindset.

I sharply exhaled, then smiled.

She continued, "Four hours is a lot, but it's what you're here for, right? Giving the ERP that kind of undivided focus and letting yourself sit with the anxiety for as long as you need to is truly the best approach to treating the disorder. So you said you have a pretty good sense of what your symptoms are, and that's terrific! I want to let you express what your symptoms are, and I'll just listen. So, by this, I mean more of the compulsions, the urges you will get to complete a behavior that you find hard to get right or that you do to step away from anxiety."

"Yeah." I put into words as many symptoms as I could stomach and that I could think of at the time. I was at ease and awake to the immensity of the opportunities and challenges I faced here at McLean. I uncovered much detail about many of the habits I lived with, knowing that nothing would be alien to her, though they may be unique.

"I feel a need to curl my toes a few times before putting my feet in my socks. I need to touch the seats of chairs and say a phrase before standing from them."

"What's the phrase? Just so I have a sense of what to look for, if you're comfortable saying it."

"Well, I won't say it correctly, so it doesn't feel like I'm doing the compulsion. So I'll just say it instead of kind of singing it melodically, which I usually do."

"Perfect."

"So, it's 'no sh-yeah, no sh-yeah.'"

She wrote that down. I explained that I said that phrase paired with almost every ritual, and I couldn't imagine not saying it, even though it was so short and silly.

"How difficult would you imagine it would be to resist curling your toes before putting on your socks? On a scale of one to ten, one being super easy, ten being I cannot resist whatsoever."

I surprised myself by giving her a three.

As we sat in the shade of the decades-old tree, I placed myself into a funnel of focus every time I answered her questions. This tunnel vision that guided me had a source I couldn't and didn't try to identify. I was inspired. I was inspired by the natural beauty, Mindy's gracious approach to this work, and her flexible acknowledgments of every response I gave. We were in a productive dance. I stepped into commitment and didn't step away from the opportunity before me.

She deliberately and plainly offered her opening thoughts. She got the correct idea that my OCD was compulsion-heavy, though I did have some apparent ob-sessions around contamination (the dust) and socializing. She expressed her views about my variety of OCD with great compassion. We agreed during that outdoor session that I would start the treatment right then by exposing myself to skipping a single compulsion. The choice was mine, but she strongly recommended one that would be one of the easiest to part with. Sitting in the comfy chair, I realized I didn't have to comb through the scrolls of my compulsions to determine the first one I would tackle. It wasn't the easiest necessarily, but it was the option that was the shortest distance from me. The answer was right beneath me.

"I'm going to try not to do the compulsion I do every time I get up from a seat: I touch a part of the seat I'm in and chant to myself, 'No sh-yeah, no sh-yeah.'"

"Okay," she said with a warm smile. "So let's get clear here. What does your OCD tell you will happen if you just get up from the seat without ritualizing?" She studied me with open eyes.

"I guess it tells me... I won't be prepared for the next moment. And I won't be able to make friends. Like, if I'm unprepared, I mean, I won't be able to... socialize, I guess."

"Okay. Gotcha. So, to start, just live with the thought that you won't be prepared to make friends. Sit with it, and just let it be there." She studied me more, communicating massive faith just with her eye contact.

"Okay? You ready to do this?"

"I think I am."

"Let's go back into the house!" She stood up from her chair and remained beside it, waiting for me to do the same, interruption-free, just as I had been able to do for years before I turned twenty-one.

Just stand up from the chair, I thought quickly. With Mindy's inviting, mirror-like eyes on me, I accepted that I wouldn't be able to make any friends. I lived with that reality, and I just stood from the chair. I felt a dark cyclone of anxiety begin to spin in me. I hadn't done any compulsions. I wandered back toward the house like a fawn finding its feet as I grinned at Mindy. The anxiety lingered for a while, but the ominous cyclone that I feared would swell diminished and soon vanished as I felt the sun on my face anew. My anxiety was replaced with new colors, new excitement, and some dribbles of residual unease.

Mindy walked with me back inside, and when I looked at her again, she had the same confident, sweet smile as if she was saying, "I knew you could do it."

25
I Deserve to Be Free

The next day, Mindy decided to take it relatively easy on me and assigned a book so I could better understand the possible origins, mechanisms, and treatment methods for OCD. Even reading the book was a challenge. I enjoyed the author's work, but spending time relaxing and reading without introducing a ritual into the mix was strongly troubling. So, of course, I did *ritualize*, a new word I picked up at McLean that described the action of performing compulsive behavior effectively.

It was triggering to read about a disorder that wreaked such havoc on my life. It would be easier to read after I had healed from it, I told myself, but I understood why I should be informed going into treatment. Still, I let thoughts that the contents of the book were stored in my left shoulder get the better of me, and I jerked my shoulder back and forth ritualistically.

At last, two hours had passed, and Mindy found me to welcome me to the next stage of the ERP session. Over time, I noticed the staff at McLean, the graduate students, the therapists, the social workers, etc., were an almost completely female squad. It was uncannily like the squad of my mother's friends who, along with their teenage daughters, all raised me in my infancy and childhood. Now, I was surrounded by powerful women embodying the mighty reputation of the hospital with unflinching dedication and a high level of skill.

While I would cycle through several of the staff members in the house during our ERP sessions, this time, Mindy was going to walk me through my first official exposure during the scheduled allotment. I decided to accept the challenge of exposing myself to the anxiety related to putting my socks on without shaking them out *or* curling my toes a few times before the sock came on.

I had been unofficially resisting the ritual of shaking out my clothing. I lived with a roommate who knew full well the signs of compulsivity and who slept just a few feet from me. If I were to stand there and shake out my clothing for hours before the day started, I would be flagrantly opposing the foremost purposes of my being here. Even a fellow inpatient like Henry held me up to a high standard just by being there.

There was one catch to not shaking out my clothing. As long as I didn't step outside, there was no risk of destroying the ground. I occasionally checked spots on the floor behind me for destruction when I walked through the house, but the inside wasn't as threatening as bringing my dust-encumbered clothing outside.

With Mindy by my side, I put myself in the genuine position of agreeing with what my fearsome thoughts proposed. *I would destroy the ground.* I went to put on my socks without curling my toes ritualistically first, yet I failed on the first try. The muscle memory ingrained over the course of a year more or less took over. Then I did it. Socks on, no curling.

The rush of anxiety crashed up against my rocky shores and felt like it could sweep away the boulders on contact, but I continued moving forward. I hadn't shaken out any of my clothing that morning; that meant I was the carrier of an unacceptably hefty amount of dust clustered in my clothing. As long as I wasn't outside, I could tolerate this. I thought I could, at least. Mindy noticed me looking at the spots on the floor that I passed, and she said, "No ritualizing, Nathan! Just live with the anxiety." I rolled my eyes and then continued following her. I feared that I was right about what was coming next. I had revealed all the details of this ritual to Mindy in our sessions, and she was smart enough to see the process through to its fully flowered form: we were headed toward the front door to go outside.

Mindy walked out into the orchard without any thought or hesitation. She glided like a ballerina, her blonde hair bouncing and her arms extended to say, "See? It's possible." She stopped when she noticed I had stopped in the doorway. She observed me steadying my breath to manage my concern. I felt as stuck as the lock on a safe for which the burglar did not know the code. I was terrified of walking any further. I started to look at my feet to see if I could see the dust, just to check. I lifted my head swiftly when I remembered a very astute therapist was watching my every move. Like a sullen teenager begrudgingly emptying the dishwasher, I made a few steps outside with my eyelids low and teeth clenched. My fists balled up as my whole spirit recoiled. I then drew an arbitrary line on the ground in my mind's eye that I could not pass. There was no existence beyond that line.

Mindy encouraged me from the orchard, "Go ahead and drop dust! You will damage the ground!" With the code still uncracked and my frustration with this fiasco buzzing violently, I stayed where I stood. I remained there for five minutes, stuck between the world ahead of me and the ease of retreating into the house. She invited me forward, saying things like "Why not?" and "I will damage the ground! Say it with me!" I inched forward, even passing the imaginary line I had drawn. I was wincing and shaking. I wasn't having a panic attack, so I figured this must be survivable. I decided the line where the cement met the grass was my new impassable barrier. I was pretty sure I meant it this time.

"I can't do it on grass! It feels too disrespectful!" I shouted over the chasm between us. "It's especially hard on natural surfaces, I'm finding out, like I'm going to destroy nature!"

"Go ahead and destroy nature!" she enthusiastically invited me. I felt like a live fish dropped onto desert sand. As I imagined the microscopic and unfavorable chemical reaction of dust meeting ground, I was unwilling to see my feared circumstance come to life.

"I'm sorry, I can't," I said under my breath, not loud enough for her to hear.

I turned around and jogged back into the house despite unintelligible shouting pleas from her. I had chosen comfort over the unknown. I buckled under the authority of what my obsession told me was safer.

Mindy said that what I did accomplish was brave and that I didn't have to conquer such a deeply embedded avoidance in one day. She encouraged me to continue reading the assigned book as a small break from the exposure work. As I sat down in a hallway of the house with my book open, I couldn't help but catch glimpses of my peers' work. Some had been there, likely, for weeks longer than I, meaning they were closer to facing their most anxiety-provoking symptom in ERP. I couldn't help but watch as one woman in her thirties covered her hands in honey. She just sat on the couch with her facilitator facing her. The inpatient just watched her hands as she resisted doing anything to wash off the honey, bathing in the anxiety that overcame her whenever she touched sticky substances. The woman had an infant waiting for her at home.

After they rang the proverbial bell to call the end of ERP for the day, I introduced myself to a middle-aged man of Indian heritage. He was a physician. I saw fear trembling in his eyes as if his terrors were so painful to live with, they made his eyes slightly rattle. Eventually, I learned more about the symptoms of this thoroughly nice man and medical hero. He mentioned in one group session that he felt he had to check the inside of his coffee mug multiple times before he poured coffee into it to check that the devil had not put a microchip in the cup to track him.

There was a young lady from Utah. She had an obsessive devotion to and fear of Jesus Christ.

I had only read about severe OCD manifesting itself in ways like the ones my housemates lived with. They were like me: when they were silent, I could tell they were battling a paramount pest within, which many neurotypical people didn't have the resources to understand accurately. Once they got to talking, they were the nicest person I had ever met: gentle, unassuming, and eager to ask about their conversational partner to get the focus off them.

Luckily, everyone at the house was friendly, but this was no cocktail party. We did not wear nametags with our symptoms on them, nor did we feel a need to inquire about others' darkest struggles, as if doing so was the equivalent of asking the classic "So what do you do?" question. Due to this unspoken respect for people's privacy, I didn't get to learn about everybody's symptoms.

Being around these people, uniting at the dinner table for group sessions, and even passing by them on my way to play video games on the couch, I felt like we were a legion of superheroes. We were the ones lucky and brave enough to come to one of the best OCD treatment facilities in the world. This super-squad assembled from around the country—one from Utah, one from Connecticut, one from Minnesota, and I from New York via California—and our superpower was saying, "Enough is enough." There were only ten of us on any given week.

The palpable perseverance in the house helped make the OCDI an incubator for focusing on the only thing that mattered to me at this time: finding my recovery from the compulsions that had taken me over.

I laughed off the handout "Why I'm Treating My OCD…" that Dr. Layton had given to me in one of our early sessions, simply due to its ridiculous typeface and colorful letters. Despite my initial disdainful reaction, its message nevertheless wormed into my mind upon first reading it. It left an enduring impact on me. At the meeting table after the day's ERP, I found myself repeating from that sheet: *I'm taking my life back,* and *I deserve to be free.*

26
Destruction Bin

To my surprise, Orchard House was not the principal residence for inpatients at the OCDI. It was a gorgeous supplementary house for the fortunate eight or so who were randomly placed there. The primary residence of the OCDI was called North Belknap. NB was across campus, about a ten-minute walk from Orchard House. I soon learned walking on grass wouldn't just be an element of my ERP work, but it was necessary if I was to attend the specialized group classes put in my treatment plan by Mindy, held at none other than NB.

Though I was able to wade into the oppressive unknown after a few days, they were not easy days. With the help of a new ERP facilitator, I inched forward into a world of aesthetics that aligned with my heart's preferences: tall trees, sprawling lawns, and spring air. But I was the threat to all of this natural wonder. The further I trod, the higher my anxiety became, and the worse I wanted to check behind me that I did not leave a massive rift in the ground that was both dangerous and an eyesore.

I went on inching, with the encouragement of my guide telling me to embrace harming the ground. My facilitator asked me to rate my anxiety on a scale of one to ten, and when I responded with a lower seven, I was trusted and welcomed to make the walk by myself.

I accepted that the remedy to my incapacitating fears was reckless action. I did precisely what my obsessions didn't expect me to do. I said, "I will destroy the ground. So be it." And I responded to my intrusive thoughts with the last action I ever expected myself to make: I moved.

About three-quarters of the way to my hoarding class at NB, my anxiety suddenly obstructed my path with a massive hurdle that seemed to sprout inexplicably from the earth. My level of concern was so high, I stopped in the middle of the empty walkway that flanked the campus road. I considered the options available to me. I could keep moving and experience disorienting anxiety that would make my whole body vibrate, perhaps continuing to affect me in the hoarding class (this was an unideal prospect). Or, I could rub my clothes with a couple of thumb swipes to feel safer and more on top of the present danger.

I chose the latter.

I rubbed my pants in a regimented way. I carried on walking.

My itch to do more was unignorable. Without thinking, I rubbed my belt to rid it of toxic dust.

The mental stiffness from following my compulsive urges seized me, and I felt like a tin man, a sensation I had lived with for years. I smiled a forced smile.

I kept walking.

I was rigidly sure of myself and armored for anything to come at me after ritualizing, but I realized I couldn't even name *what* I was so sure of.

While I was walking across campus, I refused to let my left shoulder budge, like it was made of marble. If I were to loosen my shoulder, all the energies from every show I recently watched, every book I read, and certain stimuli in the world that had been transmuted into beams of energy in my left shoulder would all be lost.

In New York, I developed the routine of shooting the energy from my shoulder onto a wall and proceeding to perform a complicated reabsorption ritual. Belmont was less isolated, less controlled, and less certain. Compared to New York, the consequences of losing all those energies by relaxing my shoulder, like the hillsides around me, were vaster. As a response, I hyperconsciously kept my shoulder locked in place.

The population in NB was more than triple the size of Orchard House, numbering around thirty people. Throughout my visits to NB for my hoarding and perfectionism classes, I considered myself smiled upon by the gods of psychiatric care that I was placed in the converted colonial home down the road and that I didn't have to spend all my days and nights within the sanitized walls of North Belknap.

The building consisted of long corridors painted pale baby blue and bathroom doors with strange vertical handles that couldn't lock. As I walked down the long hallway from the entrance to the room of the hoarding class, the walls had only posters, like the ones in Orchard House, that patients drew and taped on the walls to confront their obsessions. "I will molest a little boy," one had written on it, "I am not perfect, and I love myself," another proclaimed.

Patricia, the instructor of the hoarding class, was self-confident and probably from New Jersey. Prudence seemed irrelevant to her while it was so high on the priority list of all the class members facing her. She asked the small class, six of us, to name and delineate items we were holding onto that we could honestly do without (items like trash, trinkets, and old clothing), things we wanted to keep (which could be items we held onto for sentimental reasons but didn't use often or ever), and belongings we had no interest in parting with (our smartphones, our favorite clothing). The first two categories were candidates for being tossed.

She addressed every individual to create a plan for what to throw away and to identify why they feared throwing it away. Many described that they felt that everything they were hoarding held a high value, and they didn't want to accidentally throw a piece of trash away that was actually valuable.

When her focus came to me, I spoke from my heart, making the most of what little time I had in her direction of concentration. "For me, it's like, I'm scared of losing a piece of my personality by throwing something away. Like all this stuff is a part of me, and I don't want to lose it."

"Ah," She said. "Sounds like some emotional contamination."

Trying to play it smart like I knew what she was talking about, I only replied, "Huh."

But when I heard that term, it sat with me like an enormous meal I needed time to digest: *emotional contamination.* Before the group was over, I had to find out what she was talking about.

I asked her what the term meant. She responded, "Emotional contamination is a fear that you will lose parts of yourself in relationships with others or that you will become like people you interact with who have negative qualities by your judgment. They're nasty or greedy, and you obsessively fear that you will absorb their personality qualities. It looks like that's applying to your hoarding."

So there it was. After all these years, the warm copper wiring that had been wound around my spine at an early age and stayed wrapped there for the remainder of my youth was likely called "emotional contamination." I thought of all the miserable time I spent trying to chat with my cohorts at NYU while fearing that I was handing them pieces of myself like playing cards that they couldn't be trusted to return. But I didn't fear negative qualities; I feared absorbing all qualities: bright, charismatic, selfish, snide, humble. If a peer of mine embodied it, I trembled at the high danger that they were handing their cards to me, and they would not take them back. Over the next few days, I recalled how deep my submission to emotional contamination went. With my sister, was I afraid that I would become her? Absolutely. Was I fearful that I was loaning pieces of myself that I couldn't trust her to return? Every day. This entity that had always been a major player now had a name.

After the hoarding class ended, my housemates from Orchard House were arriving for one of the few OCDI-wide lunches held at NB.

I was glad I got to attend one of the hoarding classes before the time came to confront the items I had brought from the Boston airport in my backpack and all the trash I had created at McLean that had not seen the bottom of a trash bin. My hoarding of trash was a hindering habit that would continue to affect everybody in my vicinity, especially my roommate, if I did not improve.

A few young men who stayed at NB and I gravitated toward a spot at the long table and took seats across from and next to each other. There were no young men within five years of my age who stayed at Orchard House, so here at NB was my chance to meet some of the college-aged young men who also lived with severe OCD.

There was a guy with fast-talking spunk to the point of being annoying. I tried to keep up with him, but with his trains of thought so frantic, I couldn't easily do so, nor enjoyed trying to follow him. One friend of his seemed exclusively interested in getting to know the young women of Orchard House rather than getting to know me. I reluctantly accepted that it was his prerogative. There was a third, quieter, more athletic guy who I liked and who also attended the weekly hoarding classes. He reminded me of my beloved and deceased cousin, Mike: he had an effortless coolness that drew me in and a trustworthy quality.

He and I didn't become very close, despite my wishes to develop a friendship with him. Maybe I didn't clarify enough and communicated too implicitly that I was interested in being his buddy. Maybe what I saw in him as "coolness" was just a veneer over his turmoil. He exemplified the cataclysmic consequences that occur when someone likable is quiet. I saw much of myself in him and experienced being on the other end of an event I likely initiated for many, allowing a desired connection to go completely unforged. He confirmed my inkling that consistent quiet more often than not stymies budding relationships.

The hoarding class had been warming me up for the pinnacle of hoarding challenges: throwing away my trash. A confident graduate student studying social work who held herself with poise and demonstrated acute intelligence was paired with me to guide me through the exposure of tossing my rubbish.

I was firm in my boundaries for this assignment. I unwaveringly told her, "Okay, so today, I am supposed to throw away all this trash in my backpack, but I'm telling you right now, I am definitely not going to throw away more than one item. I can't imagine myself doing that, so I'm asking you to understand that that's my limit."

"Okay, I hear you. I am going to let you know that we are here to approach the dangers of throwing things out, and to see what happens when we deposit things you're holding onto into a wastebasket. Okay?

"Yeah, but I mean, I see throwing things away as a violent act. It's voluntary destruction, and I don't really want to take part in that."

"Okay. We're not going to reason our way there, right? We're not going to rationalize OCD away. We're going to act. So I'm going to give you some space now, and you can pick something from your bag and just toss it in. Drop it in the trash and notice your anxiety levels."

I picked out a napkin from my backpack; it was the cocktail napkin the flight attendant gave me with my soda on the airplane ride from New York to Boston. I held it and looked at it.

She asked, "What are you doing right now? What are you thinking?"

I answered, "I'm just studying it. If I'm going to throw it away, I have to know what it looks like."

She firmly encouraged me to just let it go and see how I felt.

My vision shrank to a pinhole as I placed it in the small wastebasket. Wastebaskets used to be harmless as a kid, but now I might as well have been tossing the napkin into a raging inferno. It was a bin emanating with frightening power. My blood rushed to my head, and I felt a little dizzy. "Okay, that was that, and now I'm definitely done with this."

"I want you just to sit and observe what you're feeling, watch your anxiety, and just live with it." She watched me as I watched myself.

I was a stubborn bull: "I really think it's a better use of my time to focus on another compulsion that I feel I can face rather than arguing with you about throwing away more things."

She stared at me kindly, silently. Then she said, "We're going to throw away a few more things and see how it goes, Nathan." I noticed she could feel the conviction in my words because she was no stranger to conviction herself. I saw that she was interested in converting my passion for saying "No" to a passion for saying "Yes." I dreaded crossing that line. I abhorred the idea. But she believed I could push further.

Having a person across from me who was sticking by me, being there through one of the most challenging things I had ever done, was a powerful constructor of self-belief. She showed she had faith in me, and that faith trickled right through the cracks of my cemented self-protective layers. I eventually agreed (after a few groans) to throw away one thing at a time and see how I felt. I threw away a candy wrapper.

As I went to study it sitting at the bottom of the bin, she interjected, "Nope! Let's not do that. Just leave it be, and live with it being in the trash."

I rolled my eyes in frustration.

I grabbed an empty chip bag. I paced around the room without looking at the bag, just revving myself up to do what I knew I had to do. I tossed it in. I squeezed my eyes shut, then looked at my advisor like a resentful teenager. But I was gaining my footing like I had set a surfboard under me on the wave of anxiety. I kept going. I followed a three-second rule she advised: I would not hold onto the piece of trash for more than three seconds before throwing it away. That tense tidal wave ebbed, and ebbed, and ebbed. Quick practice yielded what felt like quick mastery. I had not known this formula to apply to any other areas of life I was familiar with. I thought mastery took years and years of diligence and commitment to practice.

But this worked differently. My defenses were so non-sensical, so disparate from how I saw myself as a person, that deconstructing the habit of hoarding trash that I had enforced with such vigor over time felt more like allowing for discomfort than seeking to master a new skill. It was like unspooling a ball of yarn and living with the mess more than it was like trying to crochet without any knowledge of the craft.

Sure, I snuck a couple of glances into the waste bin after throwing away some wrappers or bags that I considered especially pretty. But I emptied my backpack of all its trash by the end of the two-hour session. The traces of difficulty in this monsoon I had survived had not evaporated completely, but now all that remained of the deluge was a puddle shallow enough that I tolerated stepping in it.

My facilitator remained sitting in the same chair she had been sitting in since the beginning. My feelings toward her covered all the bases, from indignant to offended, to forgetting she was there as I was swept up in my newfound capability, to loving gratitude, to never working with her again in my time at McLean.

Despite feeling that I had crossed an internal galaxy, her still, constant presence was the part of this process that catalyzed my courage the most. As I had always felt, *viewership is close to salvation*. This current experience extended beyond being watched. She was attentively present with me, and I was responding honestly to her. We weren't singing "Kumbaya" with one another, but the imperfect relationship we shaped was the imperfect relationship that empowered me to take one step after another.

Her presence was like a scientific anomaly, a spiritual influence I couldn't explain. I learned that a contribution doesn't have to be *explicable* to be of immense value. The indescribable can sweep us off our feet, take our breath away, and change our lives. This realization was one I never would have arrived at on my own. Once she asked me to live with the anxiety, I was doubtful. But when I understood she had authentic faith in the power of her request for me to live with my anxiety, I did so. And eventually, unbelievably, it passed.

It astonished me: I had traversed planets of will and moons of courage to get here, and I had landed. Throwing away trash was a bearable undertaking.

27
I Feel Kinda Free

The wish to experience love from new faces moved me at my core when I stepped onto a New York City sidewalk for the first time. It tormented me when I commuted to the Marin Shakespeare Company internship the previous summer. I failed in my goal to leave college with just one satisfying friendship with a fellow ETW student. My closeness with Moriah, Emily, and Electric had not survived.

Now, I was finally feeling love from and for my new peers. I was getting to know them, not the pedestrians of Belmont or the owner of the car wash in town, but the people close to me. I wasn't spraying adoration onto humanity; I was bringing my concentration to those with whom I had a real chance to build a relationship. For once, I didn't feel surrounded by mere contemporaries. My housemates were my friends.

I told Mindy about my refusal to relax my shoulder and that I extended the caution of keeping my body part locked in place even as I got into bed. I told her that my left shoulder was growing numb from lack of circulation.

"What would happen if you relaxed your shoulder?" she asked.

"If I lose track of all these energies and powers, then I won't be able to make any friendships or social connections in the future."

I had created this habit in isolation, where no one was aware of it or there to question it. Now, Mindy, as well as all my housemates, were here. And she was questioning it.

Before the session ended, she said, "Well, it's up to you. It's your own shoulder."

I hadn't thought about it like that. My shoulders, especially my left, had become primarily extensions of a repetitive thought rather than just another body part.

On my next solo trip to NB, I observed my shoulder's lack of circulation and chose to drop the tension. The relief of blood circulating to that area again reached me before the anxiety. A desperate scan of the grass around me and the hills in the distance ensued as I hunted for where my rays of energy had landed. But I didn't feel like initiating the pain that came with the complex reabsorption process of squeezing the muscles around my eyes and knocking my head back. I locked my shoulder again. I walked more. I dropped it again. I decided to march through the minefield of tangible and invisible energy and accept that it was lost to me forever.

My awareness of my shoulder's tendency to steward energy remained unshifted throughout and beyond my stay at McLean. But what changed is that I accepted living among discarded, free energy. It was always my shoulder. And now, for the most part, it was mine again.

The team at the OCDI recognized the importance of fostering good physical health along with mental health. Once a week, we residents of Orchard House came over to a building just behind NB with a weight room and a basketball court. Exercising my body despite the barriers in my brain felt incredible. Having a group to work out with and sweat with, there to push me harder, put a big smile on my face. Before doing push-ups, ab workouts, and dumbbell curls, I always started my workout by running on the treadmill.

I disliked running outside, but I loved that the set pace of the treadmill broke down my inhibitions and forced me into a velocity I eventually enjoyed. I raised my speed to seven miles per hour and did my best to let my shoulders bounce naturally. The same feet I used to tap the floor ritualistically while I washed my hands were now naturally pounding the treadmill track.

While I worked out, I listened to the album *Ye* by Kanye West, which he had just released. The song from the album that became a stand-alone anthem in my fitness playlist was "Ghost Town." The track sounded like a siren of angst. As I ran, I heard Kid Cudi crooning about trying to make someone love him but inadvertently putting more distance between the two of them in the process. With a burst, I recollected all the connections that slipped through my fingers in college. I kept sprinting. I then considered all the burgeoning relationships I could cultivate here at McLean. My running continued.

In the song's climax, 070 Shake chants about putting her hand on a stove to see if it makes her bleed. When she realizes that nothing hurts anymore, she sings that she feels kinda free. I could relate to these lyrics. I put my "hand on a stove" in ERP every day, and it didn't hurt as savagely as actively avoiding the stove. I did feel kinda free.

I had weekly sessions with a social worker who pulled up my mother via video chat to communicate with all of us in the session. The most impactful of the sessions with my social worker and my mother was one during which I shared two articles I had found online about the damages a birth child can sustain in the process of a parent adopting a new family member. I had done my research; I found credible academic sources that backed up my feelings that when a parent neglects to plan the process of adoption with the birth child carefully, the missed opportunity can increase anxiety and insecurity in the birth child.

I finished reading the articles. My mother sweetly and solemnly apologized. But it was clear, in the context of the clinical trio, that there was very little to apologize for. Libby was a family member. My mother's adoption of Libby was altruistic, and whatever mistakes she made in the process didn't affect the present format of our family. There was only wisdom in listening to each family member's perspectives and considering our roles in the unit as we journeyed forward.

About six months before my admission to the OCDI, Dr. Layton recommended I see a new psychiatrist in New York. I met with an affable, intelligent, and young doctor whom I felt I could talk to. I had avoided male clinicians up until this point, determining without any evidence that the sessions would become masculine battles for superiority instead of allowing the clinician to provide a service to me.

I told the psychiatrist about a couple of online searches I made that year that had convinced me that ingesting LSD was the chief factor for the massive deterioration of my mental health. I nervously researched the effects of LSD on the human brain a couple of years after taking the substance. I read that it builds new neural pathways between various brain segments that normally do not communicate with each other. The way I saw it, OCD had been granted new thoroughfares to the various parts of my brain that had been oblivious to its occupancy in my head.

The psychiatrist was traditional and didn't know much about psychedelics. Still, he did know enough to agree that LSD is known to forge new pathways between previously noncommunicative parts of the brain. He couldn't confirm that this was what caused the worsening of my OCD symptoms, but I was quick to subscribe to the notion that LSD had to be the culprit behind OCD's influence in my life becoming viral.

A good therapist would have challenged this concept immediately. I believed that because an experience affected me only, I was the sole authority to decide what it meant. This was not so. LSD had provided me with the best day of my life up to that point, and because of the freedom from depression and an expanded view of the living universe that it granted me, I decided I wouldn't have done anything differently.

The young doctor in Manhattan prescribed me ten milligrams of Lexapro. The lowest dose was five milligrams, and the maximum was twenty. He suggested fifteen milligrams to start with, given the prevalence of my symptoms, but I only consented to take ten. Ten milligrams of Lexapro is too low to be called a "therapeutic dose" or a dose that begins providing functional relief in coordination with cognitive behavioral therapy. I was suspicious of medication robbing me of my personality, so I drew my line in the sand.

At the OCDI, the resident psychiatrist met with me once a week. He was also male. It helped that he was friendly and forthright, allowing me to like him and see past my imaginary presumptions that we would compete to be the perfect male. In the first session, I revealed my catalog of symptoms. I didn't hold back. In our second session, he presented reasonable arguments for raising my dosage to fifteen milligrams. He referenced my episode of being unable to walk past the porch of Orchard House. He told me the medication would, in essence, cycle more serotonin throughout my brain to allow the ERP work to be more doable. I figured his recommendation was more worthy than my fear. The following morning, at the medication window next to the living room, I was handed a little plastic cup with a new pill in it. Fifteen milligrams.

When my dosage increased, I started feeling the effects almost immediately. Maybe this was another effect of having a brain that theoretically had neural pathways between its different parts. Regardless, I was able to walk further into my anxiety and strip away more of its fantastical powers.

28
No Deep Breaths

I grabbed my soap, towel, and a change of clothes. I undressed behind the closed bathroom door. Then, once I was standing in the bathtub behind the closed curtain, I announced, "You can open the door!"

During my second and third weeks, I started every day with a coached shower. These processes demonstrated how far the OCDI team was willing to go for its patients. The coach, Ashley (one of the same team members who advised us in other exposures), cracked open the door so I could hear her instructions. Once I turned on the water, she started a timer.

When I got to McLean, my showers lasted around thirty minutes. They were, to me, a famously solitary experience. Before McLean, no one could intervene in my ritualizing. With some guidance, I stood a chance at chipping away at the damaging habits I had taken on every time I washed myself. I explained to Ashley that most of my rituals in the shower were phrases I said aloud, but also included counting while washing my hair and repetitively rubbing behind my ears.

I counted to nine over and over while washing my hair. I thought of numbers usually in a dot layout, as if on the face of a die. To me, every number under ten had a distinct mood and character. Nine was as solid as they came. Five was also solid but with some distinct flair. Four was like a wheel, so it progressed forward, which I didn't care for. Three was clichéd but still reliable. Two was a beautiful pairing and difficult to use compulsively, and one represented the self.

I stroked behind my ears an exact number of times. I considered that part of my body to be the sacred space privy only to me. Before turning off the shower diverter, I had to look at all three walls and the curtain. When I lowered the diverter to transfer the water from the showerhead to the bath faucet, I felt I was giving up all my power to this lever. Thus, I delayed the inevitable as long as possible until I had to make the sacrifice and turn off the water.

The shower was an echo chamber of suffering and perfectionism. That began to change with the accountability provided by the coach on the other side of the ajar door.

Ashley had to know where I was in the washing process to do her job. Because my compulsions were usually phrases said aloud, we agreed to adapt our terminology to my situation so I didn't inadvertently ritualize. One of the phrases I used compulsively was, "I'm washing my body now, in a way… but that's not the point." So, Ashley altered her style to ask me yes or no questions.

I turned on the bath faucet and then directed the water to spray from the showerhead. Soon after, I heard, "Okay, so you're starting to wash your body now, right?"

"Yes. Chest, now armpits, legs. I really want to say my phrase."

"Just keep washing your legs and move on to your next body part."

"I think I'm going to say it anyway."

In an assertive and caring tone: "Nathan, it's up to you, but remember why you're here. To get better. I strongly recommend you keep moving on and keep progressing forward. Your goal right now is to get the showering done, get out, and not ritualize in the process."

"Okay."

Over weeks two and three at McLean, I stopped counting while shampooing. I stopped looking at the three tiled walls before getting out. I turned off the water without hesitation or delay. My echo chamber of dread became a collaborative healing experience.

By week four, I was down to five-minute-long showers. I had done it.

The menial tasks of life had become the thickest jungle I could not hack through on my own. But hearing a consistent invitation to be courageous was the wake-up call I needed.

One of the mammoth weights still bearing on my mind in week four was reconciling the energy stored in and lost through my left shoulder. I stood in the house's living room during ERP, and my advisor stood close to my right. I faced the living room wall, where there was a large window with its blinds closed. The plan was simple. I rolled one shoulder at a time, defying every wish to keep my shoulders still.

The sensation arrived with terror and punctuality: I was infusing the wall with an intolerably significant form of energy. I had been watching *Arrested Development* in ERPs to test my ability to enjoy television without shedding its contents from my body. I made my peers jealous by watching a comedy during the therapeutic work. They didn't understand that consuming any media without ridding myself of its contents afterward was a dire challenge for me.

Now, as I rolled my shoulders, I was splattering all that spectacle and the almighty energy of the world that I took in nonstop all over the wall. *Pay it no mind. Just keep rolling. Just keep rolling*, I told myself. I did just that, and in a few minutes, I broke into giggling like I was being tickled. It was so ridiculous to me that I was really doing it.

"Can I take a break to see how I feel?" I asked when my laughter diminished.

"Sure, take a break and just sit with the anxiety. No coping skills, Nathan."

I stood in awe at the shifting tides in my body and those that passed before my eyes like lapping waves coming inward toward shore. I could feel my brain's gears reorienting themselves to this new reality. It was a reality where I was releasing control, letting myself step into the ocean and accept that it could swallow me whole if it needed to.

I stood and listened to my clunking and crunching gears settling into a flow, an acceptance of the unknown. I watched all this unfold as if I were sitting front row at a tour-de-force play on Broadway. I rolled both shoulders at once—more defiance. Then, in the other direction—absurd disobedience. I tried circling one shoulder forward and the other backward simultaneously, and the play hit its climax.

I stopped again for a moment. I took a deep breath.

"No deep breaths. Just natural breathing, okay? Because it's a coping skill, you understand?"

I immediately bristled and peered into her eyes.

"This is some kind of joke, right?" I snapped. I thought, *I can tell you I'm having a problem with my shoulder, and you believe me. So you let me work on it for thirty minutes, but once I switch my focus to my own breath, you draw a line?!* I spent four years in acting school learning how to breathe well and about its powerful benefits. I was incensed.

"How am I not supposed to breathe?" I asked, eyes widening and blazing in her face. Other inpatients turned their heads toward me. I was causing a scene.

I hadn't expressed any anger in way too long. I was not used to fuming. I realized this had to say something about my emotional state: I had better access to it again.

The facilitator looked into my eyes, and in a measured tone, she explained, "We just want you to live with the anxiety you come across and accept it for what it is, not seek to get rid of it in any way." I looked right back with a smirk, unsatisfied. "I understand you might see it as just breathing, but deep breaths can ease your anxiety and become a coping skill. And we specifically don't use coping skills during ERP."

"Yeah, all right. I understand." I flicked the tip of my nose with the back of my forefinger. I had to reel in my pride; my recent successes with consistent courage emboldened me. I would be wise to follow directions here. I went back to rolling my shoulders, now more vigorously. I watched my breath—just watched it, as I naturally inhaled and exhaled. I could tell what she was talking about because now my anxiety was more gripping, more earnest. The subsequent, slow passage of it from my body felt more triumphant.

I wanted to breathe however I wanted, whenever I wanted. But the rigorous treatment here insisted upon unadulterated cooperation with anxiety, a sense of hospitality toward it, so that I could claim full credit when it eventually parted ways with me and blew away silently into the breeze.

I couldn't have accomplished what I had at McLean without stepping into the nearest access point to the woods called Rocky Meadows. The park was a few blocks from Orchard House. When I finished the day's scheduled activities, I often walked half a mile to Rocky Meadows, an access point to the woods surrounding McLean.

When I got to Manhattan, my first impression was that it was devoid of trees. Trees, grass, butterflies… they are all precious. In New York, I feigned interest in the storefronts along Broadway in search of revitalization. Here, I didn't have to feign anything. Here, I got to absorb bits of nature's powerful secrets that one can only learn by entering into it.

My time in the woods gave me the calmness I needed to reflect on the compulsions I was proud to overcome. It equipped me with the focus I needed to approach those compulsions that still clogged my right to fluidity.

29
After All, They're Only Puddles

The success I found at McLean was not a miracle. I had delinquently ignored the request of my therapist in New York to do the work she asked me to do, essentially faking my way through exposure and response prevention every week we worked together. Conversely, I didn't let up my dedication to the ERP work from the moment I got to McLean until the day I left. The mindfulness group class, in which we observed details of the nature surrounding Orchard House in silence and concentration, galvanized my mind. Rocky Meadows restored my peace. The work's collaborative design and the presence of community changed my life. There was no secret besides the most obvious one: I couldn't have gotten to where I was now on my own. And still, despite all the OCD Institute's positive influences on my life, my work was not done when I reached week six.

Every weekly session with Mindy Brooks illuminated my inner state more. She was a great listener without pretense, and I was brave in my sharing. I listed as many symptoms as I could think of so that they were all in the open and able to be addressed. All of our time together had the fat trimmed off. Our mutual focus was on being productive with our fifty minutes for my healing. I trusted her, I liked her, and I took advantage of her expertise.

It was a beautiful interplay I had with Mindy. She had no interest in slowing me down or questioning the capability I was demonstrating to extract my compulsions from my lifestyle. We used most of our time to collaborate on the strategy for whichever debilitating habits we would address each week. During one of our last sessions, Mindy welcomed me into her office, holding a tennis ball. She had learned I was struggling dearly to live with the word "genius," so Mindy suggested a simple exercise.

"I have this ball here, just a normal tennis ball, and we're going to toss it to each other. But I want to expose you to hearing and saying the word genius since you struggle with both, correct?"

"Right."

"So we're going to do this game where we toss the ball to each other. And every time you toss it to the other person, you're going to say the word 'genius.' Make sense?"

"Yeah." I grinned instinctively, then retreated into myself, redirecting my glance down as I imagined the impossibility of this exercise. Then I brought my gaze back to her and confirmed I was ready.

Once she described the nature of the exercise, I planned just to delay my response to the exposure. Delaying one's response in ERP was akin to a second-tier win, just under the first-tier win of preventing any response. In the culture at McLean, inserting some space between the trigger and the ritual was still admirable.

I was convinced I would have to do at least some light version of my compulsion after a bombardment of the word I did not say. I would do it outside the office, where there was some possibility of hiding. The cost of not ritualizing was so high. I could lose all connection to the concept behind the word "genius," one of the most profound and unfathomable concepts I had ever encountered.

She tossed the ball before I had any more time to think. "Genius," she said.

It landed in my hands. Nervously, I tossed it back. "Genius," I said.

"Genius."

"Genius," I said, a slight smile lifting my lip. But delight was not the ruling emotion here. Summoning those four frames in the air and saying a ritualistic phrase as I swung my head between them was what I was craving to do during this exercise. But I obliged the structure of the game. I proceeded without engaging in anything compulsive, dumping a bucket of ice-cold water on myself with every utterance of "genius" both on her and my part.

After around a dozen tosses, I brought in some of my acting acumen. I said the word in different tones and elongated different syllables, tasting what it felt like to have a word leave my mouth that I strictly avoided saying for a year.

Eventually, tired of the exercise's simplicity and wanting to increase the discomfort (a terrific sign of progress in ERP), I suggested to her, "What if we say the name of a person who we personally think is a genius when we toss the ball?"

"Okay! That sounds good. Let's do it."

I wanted to use the word in a sentence with some meaning behind it to see if I could handle it.

She said, "Ellen DeGeneres is a genius," and tossed the ball.

"Ralph Waldo Emerson is a genius." *Toss.*

"I think Oprah is a genius." *Toss.*

"I think Michel de Montaigne is a genius."

"I think… Serena Williams is a genius."

"Leonardo da Vinci is a genius."

After at least thirty or forty tosses paired with the utterance of a heretofore forbidden word, she held onto the ball and didn't toss it back.

She said, "You said that a lot of times, huh?" Her confidence in me was beaming from her eyes with an extra bit of glow. She was careful not to congratulate me too early because she knew I had the unfortunate freedom to engage in whatever rituals I wanted beyond her office. She knew this was a big one for me, and I appreciated her remarking that I had done a previously insurmountable activity.

My fraught relationship with that word was no secret anymore. The anonymity of my suffering had been so easily vanquished. My struggle was now out in the open.

I thanked her and left the room with an unsure, "Well, let's hope I don't do anything!" look on my face.

Once again, I walked down the hall like a wobbly fawn. A tsunami had swept me off my feet. It didn't drown me, but carried me to a strange, new land. This place was uncharted and unforgiving. I wanted to learn to tolerate it.

I was alone now. I walked down the stairs at a snail's pace and trod toward my room. Before I entered, I realized I faced a big, blank wall next to my door. No one was around, and I decided I wouldn't have clued them into what was happening in my head if they were. I was staunch that I had to escape this terrifying feeling my way.

I faced the wall and noncommittally bounced my chin from left to right, then looked in the upper right corner of my vision for one second. I felt an immediate darkening of the vibrant world I had been swimming through, and with this came disappointment in myself. I entered my room and sat down on my bed. I was alone, still, and trying to breathe normally.

I decided it was best to leave the room and be around people. Before I reached the bottom of the stairs, though, I did the same, minimized version of the ritual again while I was still moving. I felt more self-sabotage, yet I was still impressed with myself for doing so little.

Downstairs, I re-exposed myself. I deliberately looked at the DVD stored in the DVD tower that had tested my tolerance previously: a movie called *Real Genius*. I read it of my own volition. I was able to move forward. I didn't ritualize any further, and I didn't burst into flames. I was okay.

I aimlessly paced around the house, trying to see past the crimson flags flapping in my face. I had only treated two of the more than thirty utterances of "genius" with ritual. So, the flags continued to wave, warning me that I was in danger. I continued to ignore them by accepting them.

I walked outside. Evening was descending, and no one else was out there. I walked through the apple orchard and let my brain traipse the rocky path toward stasis.

I've learned uncertainty is quite like water: it falls from the sky beyond our control, fits in whatever container one makes for it, is most beautiful when unbounded, and nourishes us. Uncertainty is elemental to life.

I was in the middle of a deluge of uncertainty, and I was drenched. I had walked into a wall of water, and now I was within the storm. I had been stepping around raindrops for years. I was fully aware that the task at hand was just to soak. I walked through the orchard, and I brought to mind what I learned in mindfulness class: to notice the texture of the grass, the height of the blades. I watched the grass fidget naturally in the breeze. I went to place my hand on a tree trunk, but I knew it would reduce my anxiety, so I resisted. I just soaked.

The tempest lessened to a misting, and still I stood. The sun was setting behind thick trees in the distance. All that remained now were the remnants of my anxiety that persisted—the leftovers from the storm I had survived: puddles.

These I could handle. The deluge was behind me. Not only did I survive, but I also claimed my right just to be. The process hadn't been entirely excruciating—it lifted me with a thrill.

I felt more whole than I had in a decade.

These still puddles in the earth weren't something to avoid—they were the evidence that I had embraced a vital aspect of life I had avoided so thoroughly that I didn't even understand what my therapist meant when she used the word *uncertainty*. I was oblivious to the concept and then avoided it with all my strength. Now, the downpour was reduced to shallow pools in the earth. I realized I could handle this new coexistence with anxiety. I didn't care about getting my socks wet.

It was getting dark, so I turned around and headed back inside. The walk was nourishingly simple. The haven on the other side of the door welcomed me back into its fluorescent-lit, domestic, sweet little kitchen. One of my housemates was fulfilling their duties of washing dishes and confronting the challenges this undertaking brought them. The main dining table was half-filled with housemates playing a game of Bananagrams—a game like a deconstructed Scrabble. I felt called to the couch. I crossed beyond the game, into the living room, and plopped down on the plush blue sofa.

I looked out onto the orchard. I watched as night embraced us. I had no idea what was going to happen next. I felt perilously unprepared if something important were to occur. And it felt great. *Is this what it feels like to be ready?* I thought. I realized then that how prepared I felt was of no service to me. If Ralph Waldo Emerson were to walk through the door and engage me in conversation, then Ralph Waldo Emerson would walk through the door and engage me in conversation. I didn't have to be poised in a special way.

I sat back on the couch and thought back to when I had such a warped sense of uncertainty that I pictured it as a gray archway floating in the city, whose opening I had to approach. I laughed to myself because my recent experiences of being unsure were everything but gray. Uncertainty was as ethereal as I had feared, but accepting it and experiencing it was a powerful, nuanced, cooperative dance. Feeling what it felt like to not know infused my world with more vivacity and presence than I ever thought possible. It allowed me an intimacy with the world I never thought I could have.

Someone at the table snapped me out of my introspection by calling my name. They asked me if I wanted to play Bananagrams with them. Without thinking, I said yes.

Epilogue

There is deliberation about whether to refer to OCD as a "disorder," a "mental illness," even a "superpower," or something else entirely. I find that it is often supporters who do not live with the condition who optimistically (and, in my opinion, ignorantly) call it a "superpower." I can understand why some rooting for me would like me to see my affliction as an asset. *If you live with it chronically, you might as well embrace it!* seems to be the sentiment from several well-intending advocates.

It is my personal feeling that the experience of living with this disorder is not a superpower. Through walking the path that OCD had planned for me, by trusting its assertions and magical laws for the majority of my life, I reached the darkest depths I have ever, and hopefully *will* ever, reach.

We can all claim our power at any time, *now* being the optimal time. We all have innate, sublime power and don't need to hyperbolize it because power is enough—we don't have to be super if we're not ready to be.

On my final day at McLean, seated at the dining table where I had learned invaluable strategies for relapse prevention, lessons in mindfulness, and techniques for sleep hygiene, I was invited to speak to the rest of the Orchard House residents and a few staff members who were there with a parting message.

I began by saying, "When I first arrived here, I felt it was unfair how much we had to focus on and center our days around uncertainty when the rest of the world doesn't have to. But then I learned here that uncertainty is a *huge* part of life; it doesn't just impact people with OCD…" I looked some staff members in the eye and continued panning my head around the table, "It affects literally everyone."

I shared an insight I had discovered during a one-on-one art therapy session I did in the garden with a lovely art therapist who allowed me to use dance to help unstick my shoulder. I told her, and the room full of a dozen or more attentive faces, "What I've found here is earned simplicity."

A couple of hours later, I took an Uber to the airport and flew home to California.

Allow me to break down the ideology behind *earned simplicity*. What I found was *earned* because it took deep work to uncover it, and I was proud of my efforts. There was no need to feel any guilt that I earned my way to all-around better well-being. This state felt *simple*, quite unlike how I always envisioned betterment feeling. I saw being on the "other end" of treatment as feeling broken, thoroughly scared, and achingly lonely. But finding freedom from the majority of my symptoms yielded the greatest surprise of my life: a simple lifestyle. Wellness was not thrashing like a white-water river in its complexity or pain; it was tenable.

I don't imagine I'll find a total end to my obsessive-compulsive symptoms anytime soon, if ever. It is a chronic condition, after all.

Even after overcoming the bulk of my debilitating symptoms, OCD still does not feel like my superpower. Self-acceptance is a superpower. Courage is a superpower. The willingness to trust in the benefits of a simple life, even when you believe that complexity is necessary to achieve genius, is a superpower. Being a part of a community is a superpower.

I don't know if there have been some oversights in my representation of my own character in this book (there are bound to be); I don't know if my shoulder is still capable of placing tangible energy onto surfaces when I move it; I don't know a lot; and there's nothing super about that. But accepting these uncertainties *is* power.

Acknowledgments

Thank you to my mother for providing me with an environment highly conducive to writing this book. Sanibel has been an invaluable resource and home to create *Path Illogical*. I owe my being here to you, and I thank you for all the patience, feedback, and space you've given me. It's all empowered me to get this book published.

Thank you to my father for reading and editing the book in its earlier stages. Thank you for being a writer and editor in the first place, contributing to the genetic cocktail that puts writing in my blood. Having someone in the family who has self-published is an uncommon scenario and a source of inspiration to me.

Thank you to all the editors who put in marvelous work on this book: Larry O'Connor, Amber Hatch, Carmen Riot Smith, and Holly Welker. Especially the ladies on my editing team, you pushed the quality of this book forward and made me think about my writing in ways I never could have without your articulate and brave work.

I want to thank my uncle Matt for being an inspiring male figure in my life and for making an offhand comment that spawned the creation of this book. I don't remember what you said, but I'm glad you visited and I'm glad you said it, because I may never have gotten the idea to write a book about my experiences with OCD if you hadn't.

I also want to thank all the people I became close with in college, and those with whom I failed to become close. Your unending patience and generosity kept me safe in those years, and I thank you for not ostracizing me despite my consistent quiet.

Thank you to Laurie Gough, Betsy Hall, Teresa Bandrowska, and Brenda Overturf. Ours was the best critique group I could have discovered, and I thank you for your support and feedback, which were immensely helpful on my editing journey.

Thank you to my OCD therapists for offering your insights about the creation of this book and setting eyes on early versions of it. Without your brilliance and boldness in your therapeutic work, this book would not exist, and I would be in no condition to write about recovery. But I am, and this book does exist. So, thank you.